Uncommon Love

MARY COMM

UNCOMMON love

God's Heart for Christian Parents of Gay Kids

A Bible Study for Parents of Those
with Same-Sex Attraction

NASHVILLE

NEW YORK • LONDON • MELBOURNE • VANCOUVER

Uncommon Love

God's Heart for Christian Parents of Gay Kids

A Bible Study for Parents of Those with Same Sex Attraction

Published in New York, New York, by Morgan James Publishing. Morgan James is a trademark of Morgan James, LLC. www.MorganJamesPublishing.com

The Morgan James Speakers Group can bring authors to your live event. For more information or to book an event visit The Morgan James Speakers Group at www.TheMorganJamesSpeakersGroup.com.

ISBN 9781683509288 paperback
ISBN 9781683509295 eBook
Library of Congress Control Number: 2018930759

Cover & Interior Design by:
Christopher Kirk
www.GFSstudio.com

All Scriptures NIV unless otherwise noted.

In an effort to support local communities, raise awareness and funds, Morgan James Publishing donates a percentage of all book sales for the life of each book to Habitat for Humanity Peninsula and Greater Williamsburg.

Get involved today! Visit
www.MorganJamesBuilds.com

PRAISE FOR UNCOMMON LOVE:
God's Heart for Christian Parents of Gay Kids

So real...so needed...so relevant. At times, we see a huge hole that needs to be filled—this is one of those times. This unique Bible Study builds a bridge of hope for parents wanting to reach their SSA child through a caring relationship. My friend Mary Comm has "uncommon love"— you can have it too.

–June Hunt
Hope for the Heart Founder & CSO (Chief Servant Officer)
Author: How to Forgive...When You Don't Feel Like It

Hope, peace, healing, help, and direction are just a few of the words that describe what the Uncommon Love Bible study provides for parents whose children, of any age, have SSA or are involved in the LGBT community. Uncommon Love provides parents with a sound Biblical approach to dealing with this current issue in a practical, loving, grace-filled way in today's culture. I highly recommend this one-of-a-kind study to any parent or ministry leader who is dealing with this sensitive topic.

–Dan Schmidt
Family Ministries Pastor
Foundations Church
Loveland, Colorado

Mary Comm has written this Bible study from the compassionate and compelling viewpoint of a mother who deeply loves both her Lord and

Savior Jesus Christ and her daughter. Mary is astonishingly vulnerable about the deep pain experienced by parents of SSA kids, while also shining a brilliant light of hope through the prism of faith in God's Word. More than a Bible study for parents, Uncommon Love is a beautiful tool for Christians and churches to use in beginning a new and better conversation around the issue of homosexuality—a conversation focused on Same-Sex Attraction as the result of deep heart wounds, and our Great God who still heals hearts and transforms lives today through His uncommon love for all.

–Susan Eastham
Wife and mother of an adult son transformed from SSA
Author, Bible Teacher, Speaker
College of Biblical Studies/Houston
Dallas Theological Seminary

This study has been a marriage-changer for my husband and me. It has challenged us both to dig deep about how we really feel and then more importantly, to TALK to each other! Before this study we would just argue IF we even talked about our son. It also gave me the peace I desperately needed by knowing God's heart on this issue. Many Christians don't support parents with SSA kids; instead they judge us or alienate us because they believe the lie that this is who God made our kids to be.

–Beth F.
Bible Study Participant

Uncommon Love moved me from feeling helpless and hopeless to being full of hope as I continue to navigate this journey with my SSA child. Prior to this study I was feeling isolated. Now I know I am not alone.

–Jan R.
Bible Study Participant

Uncommon Love is replete with faith, hope, and compassion woven through every page. The message is clear: God's love and compassion reach even those caught in Same-Sex Attraction; His heart is broken for them and with them—as well as for their parents—and

He is faithful. Thoroughly Biblical; beautifully written. Uncommon Love is fresh, creative, and stimulating—written well by one who has walked this path.

–Barbara Hanno, Author
Former Consultant, McGraw Hill Publishing Company
Former Area Director, Prison Fellowship

God brought this Bible study exactly when I needed it. The study really helped me work through a lot of the questions I had. I genuinely appreciated the Biblical foundation as I was wrestling with how to hold onto truth and still be loving toward my daughter without condoning her sin. I highly recommend this study.

–Michelle B.
Bible Study Participant

For Zach and Jenna,

through whom God has blessed me
beyond all I could ask or imagine.

I love the two of you with my life,
and I am eternally grateful
for the privilege of being your mother.

All my love forever,

Mom

Table of Contents

Acknowledgements

First and foremost, I want to honor my Lord and Savior Jesus Christ. This work would never have been done, nor would it exemplify Him as it does without His calling, provision, and empowerment. This book is about Him, pure and simple—His love and provision for broken, hurting people. I am simply honored He chose to assign this project to me.

Secondly, this Bible study most likely would have never happened without the faithfulness of Dan Schmidt, Executive Pastor of Foundations Church in Loveland, Colorado. When he saw what this support group was about he simply stated, "We want to do this." He has been the overseer of this ministry and the kind shepherd of every aspect of it. He is truly the hero of this project!

Dee Feldman, Elder elect, was also a vital part of the Foundations team. She humbly took on the responsibility of assuring the theological integrity of this Bible study. Her knowledge of Biblical theology and wisdom of application were invaluable to this work, which she performed with tremendous grace and kindness. The "stranger" who went through the Bible study with a fine-toothed comb turned out to be a friend—for whom I am very grateful!

Pam Montgomery and Zach Comm both lent their time and talents to the editing process. Their skills and insights were incredibly helpful, and the book you hold in your hands is a much more refined and articulate product as a result of their expertise. Thank you, Pam and Zach, for making this book better.

Finally, my dear friends Lee Ann Delis, Pamela White, and Melissa Thompson were my prayer warriors, as well as my kind encouragers. Their love for our God and for me were evident every step of the way in this process. They were there to cheer me on, encourage me, and beat back the forces of evil as they attempted to overwhelm me. I love you girls so very much, and yes, I thank my God every time I think of you!

Each of these amazing people has played a vital role in bringing this Bible study to fruition. I am grateful beyond words to each one. I am thankful God brought you into my life—for such a time as this.

This labor of love was also one of necessity, and I am humbled to have been a participant in it. As I have begun to realize: if anything good has come from me, I owe all the glory and honor to my God and Father, Jesus His Son, and the Holy Spirit who lives within me. He is my hope, my strength, and my All in all…and I owe Him all I am.

Mary Comm

Introduction

She was beautiful; wounded. Rejected, abandoned, and thrown into the street like so much garbage. She was doing the best she could to make a living, but her best had led her down a dark alley and into serious trouble.

The Pharisees had arranged the rendezvous: a married man in a back room on a quiet street and this wreck of a girl. The plan was perfect! No one would know they were behind it all.

Did the man seduce her? Did he rape her? Did they even do "the deed" before the religious leaders stormed through the door and whisked her away, allowing the man to slip out the back door without being seen?

The ornately robed teachers of the Law dragged the woman through the streets. She, draped in a bed sheet; and they, seething with righteous indignation and a taste for blood.

Jesus wasn't hard to find. As usual, He was seated in the temple courts teaching a group of people, when the Pharisees broke through the crowd and threw the bedraggled woman at His feet. Forcefully they pulled her to her feet, making her stand in front of Him as they testified against her, demanding that Jesus determine her fate, while reminding Him of the Law concerning such sins.

The perfect trap had been sprung—or so they thought. The Law was clear in these cases. A woman caught in the act of adultery was to be stoned to death—along with the guilty man—though no one seemed at all concerned about his part in this sin. But Jesus had proven Himself to be compassionate toward sinners, so what would He do? If He allowed her to be stoned, He would alienate those who were living sinful lifestyles. But if He renounced the Law and pardoned her, He would lose all credibility and prove Himself a heretic to the entire Jewish population. The crowd had already begun to pick up the stones they would hurl at the guilty woman in anticipation of Jesus' proclamation. How could He do anything but follow the Mosaic Law?

There was no dilemma for Jesus. He knew what the Pharisees had done, and He knew just how to handle the situation. Slowly, Jesus bent down and began writing in the sand with His finger.

Deception. Exploitation. Bribery. Extortion.

But the religious leaders continued to question him, righteous anger and bloodlust dripping from their words.

Slowly Jesus straightened up and said to the crowd and the teachers of the Law, "Let any one of you who is without sin be the first to throw a stone at her." Without looking in their faces, He stooped down and scribbled in the sand again.

Murder. Hatred. Malice. Jealousy. Envy. Pride. Lust.

Recognizing their own sins in the etchings in the dust, they began to go away one at a time, dropping their stones where they stood. The older ones left first, as the younger ones wrestled a bit longer with their pride, until no one but Jesus and the woman were left there. The thud of the stones hitting the ground still rang in her ears as Jesus straightened up and asked her, "Where are your accusers? Has no one condemned you?"

Slowly, with her chin still resting on her chest, the woman raised her eyes to scan the area around them. Barely able to speak above a whisper, she replied, "No one, sir."

Gently, Jesus lifted her chin so their eyes could meet for the first time.

"I don't condemn you either," He said, His eyes radiant with love and His voice filled with gentleness and compassion. *"You are free to go; go now and leave your life of sin behind."*

℘℧

Now *that* is uncommon love! Jesus risked not only His reputation, but His life, the lives of His disciples, His mission—everything, to show His love for this woman. How many of us would take such a stand for such a woman when surrounded by our peers who were obviously not in agreement with us? Oh sure, sitting here in the comfort of your home it's easy to say, "Of course I would have stood up for her!" But would you? *Really?*

The story above, taken from John 8:1-11, is true, although many of the specific details are the products of my imaginings. This story of the woman caught in adultery has been one of my favorites for most of my adult life. So why am I telling it here, in the context of a Bible study for parents of children with Same-Sex Attraction?

The truth of the matter is that just as the woman caught in adultery was living a life of sin, she most likely didn't get there by choice, and neither did your child with Same-Sex Attraction (SSA). Let me explain.

Many Christians believe Same-Sex Attraction is a choice. They believe these people have *chosen* to be attracted to people of their same gender; that they have *chosen* to forsake normal sexual desire for an unnatural one, that they have *chosen* to give God the middle finger, turning their backs on everything their Christian parents taught them. These Christians believe it is rebellion, pure and simple. They believe those who have SSA choose to have homosexual desire, abandon their faith, and live on the wild side out of spite, lust, or fill-in-the-blank. If we're being honest with ourselves, that's what many of us believe.

Let me assure you, there is so much more to this story than what meets the eye.

On the contrary, most, if not all people who have been faced with Same-Sex Attraction have struggled with those feelings, some to the point of taking their own lives. I've never heard of anyone who recognized those feelings as a child, teen, or young adult and thought,

"Cool! I'm gay! This is awesome!" Instead, they push those feelings of attraction down, choosing to deny their feelings. They wish them away; they try to pray them away; they may even throw themselves into a physical relationship with someone of the opposite sex to test their feelings and to prove they're not really gay.

No, realizing a Same-Sex Attraction, especially for children raised in a Bible-based, conservative Christian home, is about the worst thing these kids could imagine.

Just like the woman caught in adultery, these are kids with beautiful souls and deeply sensitive hearts, who have been wounded in ways you and I as parents probably never saw or expected. Feeling alone, rejected, and even abandoned by God, these kids often tire of struggling against something they feel powerless to control. Either they give in to it, deny it as long as possible, or in utter futility and hopelessness, take their own lives. If their survival instinct is strong enough, they will do what they have to in order to stay alive—just like the woman caught in adultery. Sadly, just like that woman, they often find themselves trapped in a lifestyle that relentlessly eats away at their tender souls and chips away at their hearts from the inside out.

Finally, just like the story of the woman caught in adultery, our response needs to be more like Jesus' response than that of the Pharisees. As parents, and as children of God, isn't that what we want?

Sadly, we don't have Jesus' intimate knowledge and understanding of our child's heart, mind, or what caused this Same-Sex Attraction in them. He is all-knowing; we are not. Therefore, in our lack of understanding, we will automatically revert to what's right and wrong, to the black and white of the situation. We want to tell them: *Just stop looking at people of your gender! Just pray and ask God to take these desires away! Just confess your sin, renounce your homosexual feelings, and do the right thing! Just...STOP!*

It's a little like telling an alcoholic to just stop drinking, or telling someone with an eating disorder to just stop binging and purging. It sounds simple enough to those of us who aren't dealing with what they're dealing with. In reality, however, *"Just stop it!"* never works. Oh sure, people can white-knuckle it for a while, maybe even for a long while; but changing the behavior doesn't address the root causes. It doesn't heal the hurt. What it does, however, is to place untold pressure, blame, and shame on our kids with Same-Sex Attraction.

So what's a parent to do? Even more so, what's a *Christian* parent to do?

That's what this book you're holding is about. This is a Bible study for parents who want to love and respond to their SSA children in the same manner that Jesus would. This book is about examining Same-Sex Attraction through the lens of Scripture and with the latest information on SSA in order to understand better what our children with SSA are going through. It's about learning to love them as Jesus loves them—in their sin, in their hurts, and in their bondage to a sexual desire for which they never signed up. It's about having a better understanding of your child's wounds in order to stand in the gap for him or her for as long as necessary. That's one purpose of this book.

The second reason for this Bible study is to enable you, as a Christian parent, to maintain or repair your relationship with your SSA child. Often, without meaning to, we blow up our relationships with these kids—out of a desire to help them, out of ignorance or fear, or out of our own shame and humiliation. But just as God chose these kids to be our children, He chose us to be their parents, and the parental role is one of the most influential and compelling relationships in the universe. If you want to have influence in your child's life, if you want to have a close relationship with or her, you have to figure out how to wrap your mind around this thing she is dealing with—and in a way that is conducive to preserving trust, openness, and respect. If we disown our child—or she disowns us—because of Same-Sex Attraction, we lose the opportunity to love and support her as Jesus has called us to. Does that mean we violate our faith and condone homosexual behavior? No! Absolutely not! But what it does mean is that we have to see our children through His eyes, to love them with His love—His uncommon love—and we have to learn to deal with our own feelings about the issue apart from our interactions with our children. We have to put our relationships with our children above our hopes and dreams, but without abandoning our faith or condoning wrong behavior. Healthy acceptance in the context of unconditional love without compromising your faith will be addressed in the first chapter.

Finally, this book is about you. It's about meeting you where you are as the Christian parent of a child with Same-Sex Attraction. It's about helping you to sort out your feelings, to face your fears, to unwrap your pain, and to lay it all down at Jesus' feet—and doing so within the context of a safe and loving small group. Through this study, you will learn to experience peace in the midst of your pain and to trust God on a deeper level. You will learn to identify where you are in your grief and how to grieve in a healthy way. You will discover the best way to fight for your child instead of fighting with him. You will learn to set healthy boundaries, how to be Christ to your SSA child, and to take care of yourself along the way. You will discover how to let go of the need to control your child while never letting go of hope for his wholeness. One of the purposes of this Bible study is to give you a safe space in which to heal, to strengthen your faith, and to move forward into whatever God has for you, as the parent of a child with SSA. Whether you've been on this journey for two weeks or twenty years, or whether your child is ten years old or forty, or anywhere in between, this study is for you.

I'm not going to lie to you. This journey is not an easy one. It will most likely confuse you at times. It may even make you angry enough that you want to throw it across the room. Trust me; I get it! But if you stay with it until the end, my hope is that you will develop a deeper, more passionate relationship with God, and a healthier and stronger relationship with your SSA child. My prayer is that you will discover God to be so much more than you ever knew He was—more loving, more compassionate, more intimate, and more powerful—and that your love for and devotion to Him will be deeper, stronger, and greater than you knew was possible—uncommonly so. My heart is with you and I am praying for you as you take this journey.

In the grip of His grace & love,
Mary Comm

How to Use This Study

This Bible study is based on Scripture and holds to the values found therein. This study discusses the very hard aspects of being a parent of a child with Same-Sex Attraction (SSA) or one who has chosen to live a homosexual lifestyle. This study is not for the faint of heart. Your beliefs, perspectives, and ways of dealing with your SSA child will be challenged. If you want a Bible study that will encourage you to learn to embrace your child's homosexuality as a lifelong condition, this is *not* the Bible study for you.

However, if you are hurting, angry, fearful, or grieving because of your child's sin and how her choices have affected her, your family, and your life; if you are trying to figure out how best to love your child unconditionally without compromising your faith, this is the study for you. If you are willing to do the hard work of digging into God's Word to see what He says about the issue of homosexuality and the possibility of being set free from it, this is the Bible study for you. If you are looking and longing for hope where your SSA child is concerned, this is the study for you.

How to Use This Study

Each week you will read the lesson and answer the questions within the chapter at home. Each lesson is divided into several sections. Each lesson will begin with a Bible verse and quote, followed by a discussion of the topic. Next will be a section titled **DIGGING DEEPER:**

Journal Questions. We encourage you to purchase a journal in which to write your answers to these questions. The next section is titled **DEEPER STILL: Study Questions**. You may either answer these questions in the Bible study itself or in your journal.

The following section is titled **GROUP SESSION.** This section contains a brief synopsis of the lesson or applicable vignette, along with discussion questions to go over within your weekly group meeting. Participation in the discussion is encouraged, but not required. Our hope is that you will be encouraged to share your responses with the group because of the safety within it. If you do not feel safe in your group, speak to your group leader(s) in private and share your concerns. Safety is essential for open and honest sharing.

A Note About Adult Versus Minor Children

This study was written with parents of *adult* children in mind. If you have a minor child, your responses will be much more proactive than if your child is an adult. If your child is a minor, the biblical principles in this study will apply; however, the ways in which you handle certain issues will be different. The age of your child impacts how you advocate and intervene for him or her, as well as the boundaries you set for your child. For example, parents of adult children have little or no input regarding the choices their children make. However, if your child is a minor and still lives at home with you, you have responsibilities and opportunities for intervention that parents of adult children do not have. We recommend you seek out professional help for yourself, your spouse, your family as a whole, and your SSA child. However, be aware that, as of this writing, the American Psychological Association (APA) requires licensed professional therapists to validate, support, and affirm SSA, and homosexual and transgender identification as a part of their sexual orientation and gender equality policies.[1] As the parent, it is advisable to interview and vet mental health professionals before acquiring their services. Make sure the therapist or counselor you choose is operating on a biblical foundation and is consistent with your goals for your child and your family. (Given the new APA requirements, acquiring the services of a Certified Professional Life

Coach may be a better source for help. See *Counseling Versus Coaching: What You Need to Know* in the Appendix.)

Our hope and desire are that this Bible study will be the catalyst for you to grow in your faith in Jesus Christ as your Savior, Lord, and as your child's advocate. We hope that through this study you will be better equipped to parent, intercede for, and advocate for your SSA child. If we can be of any service to you, please see the contact information at the back of this book. We are here to help!

The Team @ Uncommon Love Ministries

Chapter One
Uncommon Love

But God demonstrates his own love for us in this:
While we were still sinners, Christ died for us.
Romans 5:8

ॐ

"He saw you cast into a river of life you didn't request. He
saw you betrayed by those you love. He saw you with a body
that gets sick and a heart that grows weak. He saw you in
your own garden of gnarled trees and sleeping friends. He
saw you staring into the pit of your own failures and the
mouth of your own grave. He saw you in your own garden of
Gethsemane and he didn't want you to be alone ... He would
rather go to hell for you than to heaven without you."
Max Lucado[2]

We opened this study with the story of the woman caught in adultery, revealing the tension between how the Pharisees saw her and how Jesus saw her. To the Pharisees, she was a worthless sinner, deserving of death—a pawn in a much bigger plot. To Jesus, she was a precious child caught up in a horrific sin that crushed her heart and tortured her soul, and what she needed wasn't punishment to the letter of the Law, but love—pure, undeserved, lavishing love. His love for this woman, stripped down and swallowed up in shame, was shocking, surprising, and unexpected. But most of all, it was *uncommon*. Did she deserve to be loved like that? No. No more than you or I do. We've done nothing worthy of this kind of love. But isn't that the point? No one deserves the kind of love Jesus demonstrated toward us, and yet it is the very reason He came; and each one of us desperately needs it. It is this kind of love, my friend, that your child with Same-Sex Attraction needs as well.

Romans 5:8 says it best of all: *But God demonstrates his own love for us in this: While we were still sinners, Christ died for us.* He didn't expect us to clean up our lives first, before He paid the price for our sins with His own blood. No, He laid down His life first, setting us free from the penalty and power of sin, telling us, in effect, that in Him there is victory over sin and new life available to us.

Examining the Heart of God

In this first week of study, we are going to look at the heart of God, not only toward our child with Same-Sex Attraction, but toward each one of us. Why? Because one of the first questions the Christian parent of an SSA child asks is: *Why, God? Why my child? Why didn't You protect him from this? Why did You let this happen to her?*

These questions from the heart of a grieving parent come with a lot of energy and emotion. And as that parent, it is vital you know without a shadow of a doubt that God is for you and He is for your child. What we *know* about God instructs us. But what we *believe* about Him determines how we process the world around us and the things that happen to us. *What we think determines how we feel, which in turn affects what we do.* That's what we're going to look at this week: who we believe God is, and how that affects what we feel and the decisions we make.

Examining Uncommon Love—Love that Shows Compassion Without Compromise

Second, we're going to look at sin, sinners, and what constitutes an appropriate response. Where is the line between showing compassion for the hurting person and compromising our faith and identity in Jesus Christ? For example, Jesus always saw the sinner as a person with a deep need. His focus was primarily on the need and how to facilitate meeting that need. For the woman caught in adultery, He defended and protected her from her accusers before He ever mentioned her sin. He saved her life, and then and only then did He mention her sin. He loved her unconditionally while she was still in her sin, while she was reaping the consequences of her sin, and well before He said anything to her about it. What Jesus *didn't* do was accept, condone, or ignore her sin. He gave her life back to her. Then, without compromise, He admonished her to leave her life of sin.

We, as Christian parents of kids struggling with SSA and/or homosexuality must follow His example. We must be willing to hold the same line of unconditional love without condoning or accepting sinful behavior in any way. The sinners Jesus spent time with did not stay in their sin. As a result of encountering the Living Christ, tax collectors, prostitutes, and thieves changed, leaving their lives of sin. The one person we know of who bumped up against Jesus' refusal to compromise without turning from his sin was the rich young ruler in Mark 10:17-31. Jesus' admonition to this young man was to give away his riches in order to be saved. Why? Because money had become this man's number one priority; it had become his idol. Jesus knew money held the most important place in this man's heart. God expects us to make Him our number one priority. He made this very clear in Mark 12:29-31. Anyone or anything that is more important to us than God has become an idol in our lives. This idol can be money, things, power, position, people, or sin. Sadly, the rich young man refused to give up his riches (his idol) in order to make God his number one priority. How did Jesus respond? He let the man walk away. He didn't run after him. He didn't compromise His standard or adjust His requirement, and He certainly didn't pretend it no longer mattered! He simply let this young man choose. As a matter of choice, Jesus let him experience the consequences.

We must be willing to do the same thing with our SSA kids. If we smooth over their sinful behaviors, pretending their sin no longer matters or doesn't bother us, we are communicating their sin is no longer that big of a deal. This behavior then leads them to assume we are okay with their sin. Without realizing it, we have compromised our faith and our identity, rescuing them from having to face their sin. Jesus always brought people face-to-face with their sin. He did so by communicating His absolute love for them, but He never glossed over or ignored the sin itself. Why? Because sin hurts us, and it hinders our walk with God.

God can and does use the consequences of our sin to convict us and to move us toward repentance—through His kindness and tenderness toward us—through the love He pours out upon us (Romans 2:4). His conviction hurts, but it does not shame or demean us. Instead, it draws us back to His heart. His conviction is the perfect plea of a Father for the heart and welfare of His child. It does not shame, blame, condemn, or judge harshly. It merely shows up as love that desires the best for the child—an uncompromising, uncommon love.

When we rescue our children from the consequences of their sin, we become a stumbling block, potentially prolonging the time our children will remain in their sin. For example, if your child insists that you attend his same-sex union, and if you refuse to do so on the basis that you cannot support or condone a union that violates your faith and who you are (your identity in Christ), then it's possible your child will sever his relationship with you. He may accuse you of being unloving, judgmental, condemning, etc. While that tear in your relationship will hurt you deeply, it will also hurt your son. This pain, for both of you, is a consequence of his adherence to sin. You are simply remaining true to who you are as a child of the Most High God. You haven't moved in your faith or identity. Your son is the one who has moved away from God and into a life of sin.

As parents, we must maintain our faith and identity in Christ even at the expense of the relationship, if it comes to that. Doing so provides our children the opportunity to come face-to-face with their sin and the consequences of staying in their sin. To compromise our faith and identity in Christ in order to make them feel more comfortable rescues them from a consequence and enables them to remain in their sin more easily. Doing so makes us an accomplice to their sin, and it diminishes our faith. How important is our faith, really, if we are willing to compromise it in order to maintain a relationship with our child? However, as we remain true to our faith and identity in Christ, we provide a beacon back to God that, hopefully and prayerfully, will be fruitful. However, it is critical that we do so in a manner that consistently demonstrates our unconditional love and concern or our child. Let him see how hard this is for you, how much it hurts you. Let him see you would move heaven and earth for him, that you would lay down your life for him, but that your faith in Jesus Christ is *your* identity, and to compromise your faith is to compromise who you are at the very core of your being.

I once believed I had to make the relationship with my child the priority so I could maintain the relationship and my influence in her life. But two things happened when I did that. First, she started to believe I had begun to accept and condone her sin. Second, God showed me how arrogant my thinking was! His question to me was, *"Do you really believe you are the only person in the world I can use to influence My daughter?"* Ouch! What's even worse was my influence had been watered down, and I was actually making it more comfortable for her to remain in her sin. I had become an accomplice to her sin.

Influence is only positive when it guides or encourages that person to abandon their sin and to return to right living before God. If we influence our children in any other way, we have made their sin our sin. What's more, if we do so in order to maintain a relationship with our child, we have placed our child on the throne of our heart. We have displaced God, and made our child an idol above Him. Compromising our faith always brings consequences, just as sin does. Stand firm and steadfast in your faith. Trust that God will honor your faithfulness by showing your child the riches of His kindness that leads to repentance (Romans 2:4). Doing so will be the hardest thing you've ever done for your child, but it is part and parcel of God's uncommon love that will manifest in us as we put Him first in our lives and seek to obey Him in all things.

DIGGING DEEPER: Journal Questions

These questions are strictly for *you*. You do not have to share your responses with anyone. They are designed to help you 'get real' with yourself and with God. Don't hold anything back when answering these questions. Dig deep. Be honest. There are no wrong answers—as long as you are being honest with yourself. I recommend you answer these questions in a private journal.

1. What do you believe about God, about His character? Not just what you *know*, but what you *believe* in your heart of hearts….

2. When your child came out to you, what was your response in regard to God? Did you run to Him? Yell at Him? Accuse Him? Did you lean on Him or turn your back on Him in anger?

3. How we respond to tragic news or events speaks directly to what we believe about God. What did your response (in question #2) reveal to you about what you really believe about Him?

4. How would you like to respond differently as you continue to grow in your relationship with Him?

5. Write out your response to question #4 in the form of a prayer to God.

6. What do you believe about Same-Sex Attraction? Do you believe it is a sin, or that they were born this way?

7. What do you believe about Same-Sex Behavior?

8. What is the difference between Same-Sex Attraction and Same-Sex Behavior?

DEEPER STILL: Study Questions: Part I

These questions are designed to reveal God's truth according to His Word and specifically in relation to your circumstances. Remember, growing in relationship with God is a process. No one has mastered it! Before you begin, set aside some time in a quiet place without interruptions. Pray and ask God to speak His truth into your heart. Then, as you look up each Scripture, read it over 2-3 times focusing on the words and what they mean. Finally, write down your responses, being honest and transparent. Again, these answers are only for your eyes. You may either record your responses here or in your journal.

1. What do these verses say about the character and behavior of God?

   a. Psalm 103: 8

   b. Isaiah 40:28

   c. Ephesians 1:5

   d. 1 John 4:8b

   e. 1 John 1:5

   f. Titus 3:4-5

   g. Psalm 149:4

2. What do these verses mean? Do you believe these things about God?

3. Who are we in Christ and why are we here according to these verses (i.e. your identity in Christ)?

   a. Colossians 3:12

    b.   Romans 8:29

    c.   Matthew 5:14-16

    d.   John 13:34-35

    e.   Galatians 6:1-2

    f.   2 Corinthians 1:3-4

    g.   James 5:14-15

    h.   Luke 4:18-19

    i.   Ephesians 2:10

4.   Where is God in regard to your child's SSA? Has He abandoned your child or you? Considering all these verses, how would you say God feels about your child and you, even in light of your child's SSA?

    a.   Isaiah 63:9

    b.   Deuteronomy 31:8

   c.   Philippians 1:6

   d.   Romans 2:4

   e.   Luke 15:3-7

   f.   Joel 2:25

   g.   Psalm 139:16

   h.   Psalm 33:11

   i.   Proverbs 19:21

5. Do you believe what the Bible says about God? Why or why not?

6. How will God's character, your identity in Christ, and His position in your child's life affect how you go forward in dealing with your child's SSA?

Study Questions: Part II

1. In your own words, what is Same-Sex Attraction?

2. What is Same-Sex Behavior?

3. When does Same-Sex Attraction cross over into Same-Sex Behavior?

4. What does the Bible say about temptation?
    a. Matthew 26:41

    b. 1 Corinthians 10:13

    c. James 1:13-15

5. Read Romans 1:18-32 and James 1:13-15. What does the Bible say about homosexuality and how it began?
    a. Is it a sin?

    b. What other sins are included in these verses?

    c. Do these verses distinguish some sins as being worse than others?

6. Homosexuality is a type of sexual immorality. According to Matthew 15:19 and Mark 7:21:
    a. Where does sexual immorality begin?

b.   What other sins are included in these verses?

c.   What does the word *immoral* mean? Can something that is immoral ever not be a sin?

d.   Taking each of these questions into consideration, what conclusion can you draw?

7.   Given the verses you've read so far, is there anything that suggests that those with SSA are "born that way?" Can you find any verses in the Bible that suggest those with SSA are "born that way?" If so, reference them here.

8.   What's the "big deal" about homosexuality/sexual immorality? Why does it matter, according to Scripture?

a.   Mark 7:21-22

b.   Romans 13:12-14

c.   1 Corinthians 6:13-17

d.   1 Corinthians 6:18-19

e.   1 Corinthians 7:1-3

    f.   Ephesians 5:2-4

    g.   1 Thessalonians 4:3-8

9. Who do our bodies belong to according to 1 Corinthians 6:19-20?

10. Think about one of the "bigger" (weightier) sins you committed sometime in your life. Now compare and contrast that sin to the story of the woman caught in adultery in John 8:1-11. According to Mosaic Law, the sin of adultery was punishable by death. Jesus had every right to allow the crowd to stone the woman. What was His response to this woman? What was His response to her accusers?

11. Did Jesus approve of her sin? How do you know?

12. Look back at the story in John 8:1-11. Did Jesus suggest that, if she didn't receive immediate victory over her sin, He would hunt her down and go forward with the stoning?

13. If the story in the Bible was about your sin instead of this woman's, how do you think Jesus would have responded to you? Would He have approved of your sin?

14. Did your sin nullify your salvation or cause Him to stop loving you? Read John 10:27-29, Romans 8:38-39, Romans 8:14-16, and 2 Corinthians 1:21-22. What do these vers-

es say about your salvation? Can sin (or anything) nullify your salvation once you have been adopted into His family? Based on these verses, can you lose your salvation?

15. What Jesus demonstrated with the woman caught in adultery and every other sinner He encountered in Scripture, was an *acceptance of the person without approval of their sin*. To put it another way, He showed *compassion without compromising* on the issue of sin. He wanted each of these people to know He loved them; in fact, He laid down His life to pay the penalty for the sins of all people for all time. How then do you believe He would want you to respond to your child with SSA?

16. What does acceptance without approval (or compassion without compromise) look like in regard to your SSA child?

A note to parents who have already crossed the line from showing compassion for your child to compromising your faith: We recognize that this chapter may have been especially difficult for you if you have compromised your faith in order to maintain your relationship with your child. Please know God sees your heart, and He knows you did so with good intentions. Perhaps you had never been faced with the concepts in this Bible study. Maybe you never considered what doing so might have communicated to your child about your faith, or how it may have rescued them from some of the consequences of their sin. God sees! He knows! He understands! There is now no condemnation for you in Christ Jesus (Romans 8:1)! It's never too late to share your heart with your child, letting them know that you unknowingly crossed your own boundary without realizing it, and why you did so. Let them see your heart. Let them see your pain. Know also it is never too late to tell your child how much your faith means to you, or to move the boundary line. Tell her again how incredibly much you love her and that your relationship with her means the world to you, but you can no longer violate your own identity in Christ. Let him know you love him no matter what, but that you have to follow your conscience. Let him know you respect his choices even if you don't agree with them, and ask for the same respect in return.

APPLICATION: Write out your takeaway.

_____

_____

_____

_____

_____

_____

_____

_____

_____

_____

_____

_____

_____

_____

UNCOMMON LOVE

*"But God demonstrates his own love for us in this:
While we were still sinners, Christ died for us."*

Romans 5:8

৪০৫৪

*"He saw you cast into a river of life you didn't request. He
saw you betrayed by those you love. He saw you with a body
that gets sick and a heart that grows weak. He saw you in
your own garden of gnarled trees and sleeping friends. He
saw you staring into the pit of your own failures and the
mouth of your own grave. He saw you in your own garden of
Gethsemane and he didn't want you to be alone ... He would
rather go to hell for you than to heaven without you."*

Max Lucado[3]

Whenever a Christian parent hears the words, "I'm gay," from their child, time stands still for a moment. You have to remember to breathe. Suddenly, it's as though a tsunami has leveled your life, leaving everything and everyone around you looking different, unfamiliar.

Your first thought is "WHY, GOD?" Why *this*? Why *her*?

As the weeks roll by, you begin to wonder, did I ever really know this child? The person standing before you looks the same outwardly, but you wonder what happened to the child you knew before….

If we don't have a firm foundation of faith in who God is, where He is in our child's life, and in our lives, this single event could be our undoing. That's why it is vital for us to have a good understanding of who God is, who we are in Him, and where He stands in this new reality with our SSA child.

When it comes to understanding these things, we may be surprised by the intensity of our feelings toward God, our accusations of Him, or our belief that somehow He has betrayed and abandoned us. How we respond to the tragedies in life reveals how much we truly believe what the Bible says about God. However, the good news is that by His grace and through His Spirit, our faith in Him can grow.

Discussion questions:

1. What did you learn about yourself and your perspective of God through this lesson?

2. Were you tempted to accuse or blame God for your child's SSA?

3. Are you still struggling with those feelings? Why or why not?

4. Regarding the Scriptures about homosexual behavior and sexual immorality, do you believe, as the world does, that these people are "born" with SSA? Why or why not?

5. According to Scripture, where does homosexual desire begin?

6. According to Scripture, is SSA a sin? Is homosexual behavior a sin? What is the difference between the two?

7. According to Scripture, is homosexual behavior a sin that may nullify a person's salvation?

8. What other sins were listed in some of the verses you looked at pertaining to sexual immorality?

9. Why is homosexuality/sexual immorality wrong, according to Scripture?

10. What does healthy acceptance look like, according to Scripture (John 8:1-11) What does that mean in regard to your acceptance of your child with SSA?

11. If you have already crossed the line between showing compassion to your child and compromising your faith and values, how did this lesson impact you?

12. What questions from the lesson were most meaningful to you?

13. Your takeaway: If you were to sum up the impact of this week's lesson in one concise thought, what would that be?

14. Do you have any prayer requests pertaining to your child's SSA you would like to share?

Closing Prayer

Father God,

Thank You so much that You are a good God, faithful and true, and that Your love for us never wavers, never diminishes, and never ends! Thank You that nothing—not even our sin—can separate us from Your love or nullify our salvation. Thank You that once we belong to You, we are always Yours—no matter what!

Father, we lift our children to You, asking you to speak to their hearts, to draw them back to You, to replace the lies of the enemy with Your Truth. Remind them and us that You are always good even when everything around us is going horribly wrong. Help us not to accuse You of being unkind or uncaring, or to let the enemy establish any foothold in us that would cause us to question Your character. Thank You for loving us and sending Jesus to pay for our sins while we were still sinners.

In His Mighty Name we pray,

Amen

Chapter Two

The Nature of SSA

"For although they knew God, they neither glorified him as God nor gave thanks to him, but their thinking became futile and their foolish hearts were darkened."

Romans 1:21

ഇരു

"There is no such thing as "gay;" there are only hurt children looking for love."

Richard Cohen[4]

How did my kid develop Same-Sex Attraction? It's a question every parent asks when their child comes out. Did I do this to him? Was I too hard on her? Did I not spend enough time with him? We raised her in a Christian home; how could this happen? As we begin to unravel the knots in which your heart may be tied up, know you are in a safe place to put voice to your fears. But also know exploring these questions may or may not bring you relief. Hopefully by doing so, you may be able to get to the point of being okay not knowing. Whatever the case, this week's lesson will no doubt be difficult.

Let's begin by defining exactly what SSA or Same-Sex Attraction is, from a technical and practical standpoint. Regardless of what 'the world' says, SSA is an attachment disorder. In the purest sense, SSA is a heart wound pertaining to the child's ability to feel as though he belongs. Put another way, these kids experienced repeated and varied situations where they felt they didn't belong or didn't bond in a normal, healthy manner. It's a wound that goes to the core of your child's identity. Repeatedly or consistently feeling like the odd one or the 'square peg in the round hole' with the same-sex parent or peers causes the child to not just *feel* different, but to believe in their minds they *are* different. The more they believe or feel this way, the more solidified that identity becomes. Consequently, others then begin to reinforce that identity by rejecting them and treating them as though they are different and don't belong. Further, as puberty explodes onto the scene during what is already a time of feeling weird and not fitting in, their insecurities mount, cementing the notion that they simply aren't like the other girls or boys. Sadly, for many of these children, the die is cast, and we as parents don't have a clue of the wounds that have silently scarred their young hearts and minds.

A Different Type of Grief Cycle

Richard Cohen, author of *Gay Children, Straight Parents: A Plan for Family Healing* came out of the homosexual lifestyle and is now a Christian Therapist. In his book, he shares ten factors that are believed to contribute to a child developing Same-Sex Attraction. As you read through these ten factors, think about your SSA son or daughter's childhood experiences, behaviors, or attitudes, and make a note of those that seem pertinent:

1. **Heredity**: As in, inherited wounds, unresolved family issues, etc. For example, showing preference for one child over another, a predilection for rejection, destructive generational sins, etc. (not as in genetic causes or that they were born this way)

2. **Temperament**: e.g. Hypersensitivity, high maintenance, artistic nature, gender nonconforming behaviors, high empathy, codependent behaviors, etc.

3. **Hetero-emotional wounds**: Enmeshment or emotional entanglement with the opposite-sex parent; imitation of opposite-sex parent; feeling or sensing the parents wanted him or

her to be born the opposite sex, then modeling that gender to please or win the parents' approval

4. **Homo-emotional wounds**: Lack of emotional attachment between father/son or mother/daughter; abusive treatment and/or perceived emotional unavailability by the same-sex parent

5. **Sibling wounds/family dynamics**: Put-downs, abusive treatment (physical, emotional, verbal, sexual), name-calling, feeling inferior to other siblings

6. **Body image wounds**: being a late bloomer; having physical disabilities or illness; a girl who is athletically developed or gifted; a boy who is athletically challenged; children who are unusually short or tall, thin or overweight; kids with poor coordination—anything to make them feel inadequate about their physical person; (a.k.a: gender inadequacy)

7. **Sexual abuse**: especially in conjunction with a lack of warmth from the same-sex parent and/or same-sex peers. In these instances, sex becomes a replacement for emotional and relational intimacy

8. **Homo-social wounds**: name-calling, rejection by peers (especially same-sex peers), mocking over appearance, disability or anything that makes the child stand out as different than the other kids

9. **Cultural wounds**: Social indoctrination by media, educational systems, political organizations, entertainment, academia and the Internet; indoctrination that they are "born gay and cannot change"; trendiness of being gay; children growing up in single-parent homes without the same-sex parent

10. **Other factors**: Divorce, the death of a parent, adoption, religion, race, etc. can affect the sensitive child's sense of rejection, insecurity, etc. Those with an already fragile sense of gender identity will be more affected by these things.

An important thing to know regarding each of these factors is these children are often incredibly sensitive emotionally. They are deep feelers, often displaying compassion and emotional sensitivity at an early age. This emotional hypersensitivity can lead them to *perceive* offenses or infractions when none exist. Therefore, even if you never saw events or situations in your child's life as described in these 10 factors, the likelihood is your child *perceived* them. If this is indeed the case—and it often is with these children—*their perception, not your reality is what is most important*. If your child perceived rejection, criticisms, being left out, feeling different, etc., his feelings are what matters. To him, those offenses, those wounds, were his reality.

Of course, we can't know with certainty which of these factors, if any, definitively caused the child in question to develop SSA. However, making these observations can certainly give us some possible clues. Further, if you will notice, most of these wounds are completely outside the control of the parent. Therefore, if you have been wrongly blaming yourself for your child's SSA, this exercise can be helpful. On the other hand, if you feel God is convicting you of one or more of these areas of wounding, take the time during this lesson to do business with Him in those areas.

DIGGING DEEPER: Journal Questions

1.   Which, if any, of the ten factors listed above have a ring of truth in regard to your son or daughter's childhood? Identify those circumstances and journal what you observed.

2.   Of the factors you identified, make a note of which ones were or were not in your control at that time. NOTE: Be cautious in your assessment of responsibility; take into consideration who you were at that time and what was going on in your life. Remember that hindsight is 20/20. Do not judge yourself based on who you are now or your life situation today. Offer yourself grace for things you may have missed unintentionally.

3. If you feel God is convicting you of something you did or did not do at that time, take ownership of it, repent before God, ask Him to forgive you, and accept His forgiveness. Allow His forgiveness and grace to pour over you, removing any and all guilt or shame in relation to those circumstances. Know that once you have repented, His forgiveness is complete.

4. If your child is an adult, and if your relationship is strong and in a good place, <u>prayerfully</u> consider asking him or her about the factors you identified in a *generic* manner. For example, <u>DO NOT</u> ask, "Did ____ cause you to be gay?" Instead, ask, *"When you were in grade school or middle school, did you ever feel like you didn't fit in?" "Were you ever bullied in school?" "Did you ever feel like I wasn't there for you, when you were growing up?"* If your child answers yes to any of these questions, let them know you are sorry they experienced those things. Show genuine empathy or compassion. If they confirm they felt neglected, wounded, etc., by you, <u>DO NOT defend yourself</u>. Instead, own it, apologize for it, and ask for their forgiveness, letting them know it's okay if they are unable to forgive you right away. These conversations, done in a spirit of compassion, love, ownership, and forgiveness can go far in increasing the bond between you and your child. Again, I cannot stress enough that you must pray before having this conversation, asking for God's wisdom and for His heart to strengthen your own. Journal about this experience, before and after the discussion.

DEEPER STILL: Study Questions

1. Read Romans 1:18-32. According to these verses, where does homosexuality begin (verse 21)?

2. What does the phrase "God gave them over" mean, in verses 24, 26, and 28? To what did He give them over?

3. In verse 25, what did they exchange? What was the lie?

4. Homosexuality is a type of sexual immorality. According to Matthew 15:19 and Mark 7:21:

5. Why is sin such a bad thing according to Hebrews 9:28?

6. According to John 8:44, who is the father of lies? What is his end goal?

7. In John 10:10, who is the "thief?" What did he come to do?

8. Before Jesus began His ministry, He was led into the desert, where He fasted for 40 days and nights. At the end of those 40 days, "the tempter" came to tempt Jesus. Read the story in Matthew 4:1-11. What is another name for "the tempter?"

9. Jesus was tempted to sin but did not sin (2 Corinthians 5:21). What does this imply about SSA versus Same-Sex (Homosexual) Behavior?

10. What was Satan's very first line of attack (Matthew 4:3)? (Hint: It had nothing to do with bread....) How is this consistent with a child who develops a Same-Sex Attraction?

11. If your child has trusted Christ for his salvation, who does God say he is? What is your child's true identity?
    a. Romans 8:15-17

    b. 2 Corinthians 5:17

12. In contrast to Satan (the father of lies, deceiver, and tempter), and according to John 8:31-32 and 18:37, Jesus came to do what?

13. Taking all of these factors into consideration, can you conclude that your child was born with SSA or not? Why or why not?

APPLICATION: Write out your takeaway.

_____

_____

_____

_____

_____

_____

GROUP SESSION:
Chapter Two
THE NATURE OF SSA

"For although they knew God, they neither glorified him as God nor gave thanks to him, but their thinking became futile and their foolish hearts were darkened."

Romans 1:21

಼ೋಌ

"There is no such thing as "gay;" there are only hurt children looking for love."

Richard Cohen[5]

Jesus' first priority as He prepared to begin His ministry was to glorify God. Indeed, He would prove to be unshakeable on that point throughout His time on earth. His heart was beyond Satan's reach, but that didn't stop Satan from trying. When Jesus was at His *most vulnerable*—having had nothing to eat or drink for 40 days—Satan saw his opportunity to corrupt Him. Before uttering the first temptation, he questioned Jesus' identity. *"If you are the Son of God...."* With seven simple words, *Satan attacked Jesus' identity*.

When your child was young and at his *most vulnerable*, Satan began *attacking his identity*.

This similarity is no coincidence. It is a pattern. And it is astounding.

When a child embraces her Same-Sex Attraction, after years of feeling different, not belonging, not bonding with those like her; the wounds in her heart have piled up, and SSA becomes the defining characteristic of her identity. However, if your child has given his life to Christ, his identity is in Him; that's where the word *Christian* comes from. Technically, it means 'follower of Christ.' However, when we gave our lives to Christ, we didn't just sign up to follow Him. We gave our lives over to Him, becoming a new creation in Him; obtaining a *new identity* as a *child of God*. The picture in 2 Corinthians 5:17 is that of a caterpillar who comes out of the cocoon as a butterfly through the process of metamorphosis. That butterfly can never again be a caterpillar. It can behave like a caterpillar if it so desires; it can walk along a branch or on the ground, but doing so doesn't make it a caterpillar again. It is now and forever will be a butterfly. That is its permanent identity, just as our permanent identity is *child of God*.

Satan, the enemy of our Lord and Savior Jesus Christ, is also *our* enemy. He is the father of lies, a deceiver, and he hates that we now belong to the family of God. He cannot steal our salvation from us. However, if he can deceive our hearts and minds, wounding us along the way, he can destroy our witness, and subsequently destroy our lives. What an effective strategy Satan employs!

Add to Satan's strategy that our society not only embraces homosexuality, but also celebrates and promotes it. So yes, even the world around our children is working against them.

BUT GOD...! But God has proclaimed that with Him, all things are possible, and that He has overcome the world (Matthew 19:26, 1 John 4:4)! Though the enemy has deceived your child, if she is a child of God, rest assured that God will never forsake her. However, if she has not yet trusted Christ for her salvation, *there is still hope*. Do not lose heart! Though this journey is long and you may just be getting started, you can trust that the Most High God has got *you*, He's got *your child*, and He's got *this!*

Discussion questions:

1. Were you surprised that homosexuality/SSA begins in wounds in the heart? What does that mean, then, in regard to SSA being a choice? At what point does choice enter in?

2. Can someone have SSA and not sin? Why or why not? What would that look like?

3. Were you able to identify behaviors or events in your child's life (from the ten factors) that may have wounded his heart concerning attachment, belonging, or appropriate gender identification? Which ones?

4. Did you ask your child about any of the possible woundings you saw in those ten factors? If so, how did that go?

5. Does it make sense to you? Do you see the connection between a heart repeatedly wounded by not belonging, not bonding, feeling rejected, lack of appropriate attachment, etc., that could cause the child to begin to attach in unhealthy ways? Ways that lead to SSA? Why or why not?

6. Given that Scripture discussed other seemingly "lesser" sins in the same manner as the sin of homosexuality/sexual im-morality, how does that instruct us when it comes to dealing with those who are involved in homosexuality?

7. Does Scripture's handling of all these sins in the same manner diminish the weight of the sin of homosexuality? Why or why not?

8. What other factors from the study contributed to your child's SSA?

9. Has Satan ever attacked your identity in Christ? If so, how?

10. Does awareness of that change your perspective of your child's SSA identity?

11. What questions from the lesson were most meaningful to you?

12. Your takeaway: If you were to sum up the impact of this week's lesson in one concise thought, what would that be?

13. Do you have any prayer requests pertaining to your child's SSA you would like to share?

Closing Prayer

Father God,

We are learning so much about SSA and homosexuality. Help us to process this information with the guidance of Your Spirit. Guide us into Your truth, Father; give us understanding, and with that understanding, give us compassion for our children. Help us to see them as You see them—as people who, because of their wounds, are tempted to make bad choices. Some of them already are making awful choices— choices that can never be undone. We pray for Your hand of protection over our children. We pray You would lead them home, just as the Good Shepherd carried the lost little lambs home on His shoulders. Give us Your heart toward them, Father, no matter what circumstances surround them. Help us to love them as You love them, to forgive them for the hurtful things they say sometimes, and for the pain their sin costs us. Thank You, Father, that You never give up on any of us!

In the Mighty Name of Jesus,

Amen.

Chapter Three

FINDING PEACE IN THE PAIN

"So do not fear, for I am with you;
do not be dismayed, for I am your God.
I will strengthen you and help you;
I will uphold you with my righteous right hand."

Isaiah 41:10

ഇൗങ

"The secret is Christ in me, not me in a different set
of circumstances."

Elisabeth Elliot

In the mid-1950's, as young missionaries, Elisabeth Elliot and her husband Jim lived among the Auca Indians in Ecuador, an unreached people group. The Elliot's were serving alongside four other missionary families to bring the gospel to the Aucas in their own language. As it would happen, the very people they had come to share the gospel with murdered Jim and the other four missionary men.

I can't begin to imagine how horrible that experience was for these young wives and mothers. They had surrendered their lives to serve God on behalf of these people, only for them to slay their husbands in cold blood.

Their husbands' deaths, however, were only the beginning of the story. Elisabeth and the other widows remained in Ecuador where they continued their husbands' work, sharing the gospel with the Aucas, and leading the very people who killed their husbands, among many others, to salvation in Jesus Christ. The resulting transformation of this people-group as a result of these women's dedication in service to their Lord and Savior, created an influx of young Christians likewise choosing to serve God on the mission field.

How in the world did they stay and minister to the men who killed their husbands?

Strength like that is beyond rare, and I think Elisabeth Elliot would say that trusting God in the midst of her pain, loss, and fear was the only way she could do what she did. As an act of her will, out of love for her God, she relinquished control of the situation, her need for retribution, and her desire for safety for herself and her children to the one she had committed to serve. In doing so she learned to live in the strength of His peace, no matter what.

Elisabeth went on to write over twenty books before her death at the age of 88. One of the most poignant of her works is simply titled, *Keep a Quiet Heart*. It is a series of vignettes about experiencing peace in the midst of unspeakable chaos and pain.

This week, we are going to look at how we, as parents of children with SSA, can likewise experience peace amid our own pain, grief, loss, and uncertainty.

The 5 R's of Finding Peace in Any Situation:

Like happiness, peace comes down to making a choice. Following are five steps to learning to live in God's peace no matter what.

1. **Recognize** that God is Lord over all things. Nothing escapes His notice or His sovereignty. Our God spoke this vast universe into existence. Out of the expanse of nothingness, He created our world and the universe beyond—with all its beauty, massive size, energy and order—by merely *speaking* it into being. It is a living world, teeming with countless peo-

ple, creatures, and other living things, not one of which escapes His notice or acts without His permission. Everything in this universe and in your life is sifted through His hands. Every person, every act, every event was known about by Him before the beginning of time. Nothing is beyond His control or His ability to redeem, restore, repair, or rebuild. He is God. He is good. He is trustworthy. Recognize and worship Him for who He is.

2. **Respond** calmly, with confidence in Him. Your first response is to *place your confidence in Him.* As you place your confidence in God concerning the situation, your next step is to detach emotionally from the things in the situation that are out of your control. *Healthy Detachment* is a process of determining what you can and can't control, doing what you can regarding the former, and letting go of the latter, leaving it in God's hands. This determination is first made by asking yourself: *How much of what's happening is about me? How much is about the other person?* If it truly concerns you, do what you can or must in order to remedy the situation. Apologize, ask for forgiveness, and commit to not repeating that mistake again. On the other hand, if it's not about you and it's all about the other person, let her get out her emotions while holding a safe space for her. Holding a safe space simply means letting the other person get all their hurt, angry emotions out without retaliating, fixing, judging, or commenting. Just let them feel what they feel, and be there for them with empathy, compassion, support, understanding, and affirmation. As you interact with that other person, healthy detachment requires that you ask yourself: *What is the other person* really *saying?* It is committing to listening well to what he is saying, confirming with him what you've heard in order to verify your understanding, and even listening to what he *isn't* saying. For example, is there an underlying

hurt you see in his face that he's not talking about? Healthy detachment is stepping out of the fray in that moment and taking an emotional step back in order to gain a more objective perspective. It is moving out of the emotional intensity and striving to gain a non-emotional view so as to be able to respond without a knee-jerk response, but instead, with a peaceful, grounded response. Place your confidence in God and experience His peace before you respond.

3. **Remember** I AM is with you, that nothing is beyond His reach or ability to restore, rebuild, repair, or redeem for HIS glory. He has promised never to leave or forsake you (Deuteronomy 31:8). REMEMBER: ALL events serve His will (Romans 8:28). Make it a point to rehearse these statements daily in order to embed them in your heart.

4. **Release** the entire situation or set of circumstances to God by talking with Him about it. Surrender your rights to have your way in this situation. When we try to manage the situation, or manipulate circumstances or people, we become a stumbling block and we muddy the waters for that person; but when we get out of the way by surrendering the situation to Him, the way is clearer for God to work and for them to respond. Get out of God's way by releasing the situation to Him.

5. **Rest** in Him, knowing He's got *your child*, He's got *you*, and He's got *this*. In that moment, affirm this statement out loud, if necessary. "He's got *(child's name)*. He's got *me*. He's got *this*." Take a few deep breaths and rest in His sovereignty and His ability to do what you can't.

Healthy detachment allows you to continue responding as the adult/parent, with calm confidence, instead of responding out of emotional overload because of the intensity of the moment. Putting this process into practice will keep you from saying things you will later regret, things you can never take back.

DIGGING DEEPER: Journal Questions

1. What is your greatest fear regarding your SSA child?

2. How does that fear affect you? Your child?

3. What does it mean in your situation to surrender your son's SSA/life choices to God?

4. Surrender begins with a choice. If you choose not to surrender your daughter to God, how might you get in His way?

5. What is it that makes it difficult for you to trust God with your child's life, choices, etc.? What steps can you take to help you get past that thing?

6. How would using Healthy Detachment change your relationship with your child?

DEEPER STILL: Study Questions

1. What did Jesus tell us He left for us? How do we not let our heart be troubled? John 14:27

2. Philippians 4:6-8 gives us clear instructions about how to experience Christ's peace. Fill in the blanks below:

   a. Present_____ by
   _____ and _____ ,
   and with_____
   in_____ situation.

   b. Think on whatever is:_____

   1) _____

   2) _____

   3) _____

4) _____

5) _____

6) _____

7) _____

c.   The result will be that, the_____of God, which transcends all _____, will guard
your_____ and your _____
in Christ Jesus.

3.   According to Romans 5:1-5, what purpose is there in
suffering?

4.   According to that same passage in Romans, what is the end
result (verse 5)?

5.   Romans 15:13 says that God is the God of hope. What do we
need to do, according to this verse, to obtain peace, over-
flowing hope, and joy?

6.   Learning to experience God's peace is a process; it doesn't
happen overnight. It is a day-by-day, and sometimes, mo-
ment-by-moment exercise. Write out your thoughts about
this process below or in your journal. Does it feel too hard?
Is it worth the effort? What difference could peace make in
your life? In your relationship with your SSA child? What
support do you need in this area?

APPLICATION: Write out your takeaway.

_____

_____

_____

_____

_____

_____

_____

_____

_____

_____

_____

_____

_____

_____

_____

_____

_____

_____

_____

GROUP SESSION:
Chapter Three
FINDING PEACE IN THE PAIN

"So do not fear, for I am with you;
do not be dismayed, for I am your God.
I will strengthen you and help you;
I will uphold you with my righteous right hand. "
Isaiah 41:10

৯০০৪

"The secret is Christ in me, not me in a different set
of circumstances."
Elisabeth Elliot

The process of learning to walk in God's peace—especially in light of the hurt, loss, chaos, and uncertainty of having a child with SSA—is a challenging one. However, as the renowned author, Oscar Wilde said, *"If a thing is worth doing, it is worth doing well. If it is worth having, it is worth waiting for. If it is worth attaining, it is worth fighting for. If it is worth experiencing, it is worth putting aside time for."*

Colossians 3:23-24 says it a little differently: *"Whatever you do, work at it with all your heart, as working for the Lord, not for human masters, since you know that you will receive an inheritance from the Lord as a reward. It is the Lord Christ you are serving."* That verse puts a little different spin on it, doesn't it?

If we're being honest with ourselves, most of us want peace for ourselves, first, and second, to improve our relationships with our kids. Further, the reason that obtaining God's peace is so difficult, is because it means we have to give up our rights—to have what we want, to try to control the situation, to manipulate or finagle however we need to in order to get what we want. What we want is for our kids to give up their SSA lifestyle and go back to being heterosexual, right?

Here's the rub: *we are here on this planet, not for ourselves or for what we want. We are here for God's glory and purposes.* He has bought us with a price—the price of His own Son's shed blood that paid for our sins so that we could have a relationship with God, and so that we could spend eternity with Him (I Corinthians 6:20). We get the benefits of salvation: forgiveness, relationship with God, His Spirit within us, His power over sin, freedom from the things of this world that are meant to destroy us—and He gets *us*. Honestly, I think He got the short end of this stick! ;) Seriously, that was the deal when we surrendered our lives to Him.

Here's the best part: because God did not intend for your child to have SSA, and because homosexual behavior is a sin rooted in deep heart wounds, that means her SSA is not His will. This also means that God's best for your child is to be set free from SSA. Because you belong to Him, He can use your life—His Spirit working in and through you—to accomplish that goal. Here's the thing. *You have to cooperate with Him.* You and God want the same thing; but He wants you to trust Him, and to walk in His peace within the context of your life and relationship with her. That means you have to take your hands off, move out of His way, give up your way of doing things (control, manipulation, judgment, criticism, etc.) and let Him do what He needs to do. Now does that mean you don't do anything? No, absolutely not! Your job is to do what He tells you to do, to say what He tells you to say, to be silent when silence is needed, and to leave the results in His hands.

Discussion questions:

1. Learning to walk in God's peace is hard. Is it worth it to you? Why or why not?

2. What difference could peace make in your life? In your relationship with your child?

3. Letting go of control and of the eventual outcome is also really tough. Have you been able to do that? If so, how did you accomplish it? If not, what is standing in the way?

4. Do you believe God is trustworthy? Why or why not?

5. What does this phrase from Philippians 4:7 mean: "peace that transcends understanding?"

6. Have you ever experienced that kind of peace? If so, tell about that experience.

7. Faith in God is built as we face hardships and as we see how God has gotten us through those times. Have you experienced that kind of growth in your faith? Explain.

8. Would our faith grow without hardships? If so, how? If not, can we then thank God in the midst of our hardships?

9. If we can thank God in the midst of hardships, how might that change us? (Philippians 4:6-7)

10. What support or accountability do you need in the area of trusting God and walking in His peace?

11. What questions from the lesson were most meaningful to you?

12. Your takeaway: If you were to sum up the impact of this week's lesson in one concise thought, what would that be?

13. Do you have any prayer requests pertaining to your child's SSA you would like to share?

Closing Prayer

Father God,

We long for Your peace to carry us and to sustain us, every day, every night. Fear and worry come easily—too easily! Too often they crowd out peace, causing us to worry and fret over so many things over which we have no control. Father, we surrender our worry to You, today, asking You to replace our worry with Your peace that passes all human understanding; peace that is so visible to others they will ask us what happened to change us so dramatically! Let our lives be a testimony of Your peace, Your power, Your goodness and mercy. Show us when we are allowing the cares to creep in again, and give us the wisdom, discernment, and strength to cast our cares on You. Help us to believe—to know that we know that we know—You are for our children and for us, and that You've got them, You've got us, and You've got this! Thank You for providing everything we need to sustain us on this journey. You are such a good, good God!

In the Mighty Name of Jesus,

Amen.

Chapter Four

The Path of Grief

"The LORD is close to the brokenhearted and saves those who are crushed in spirit."

Psalm 34:18

൧൦ൽ

"Finding out about a gay child is agony.
It's almost like having a death in the family.
But when someone dies you can bury
that person and move on with your life.
With homosexuality, the pain seems never-ending."

Barbara Johnson, *Where Does A Mother Go to Resign?*[6]

Grief. It's a hard word with which to live. The loss of a marriage and what you thought would be a lifelong partner through divorce. The loss of a young child. The death of parents. Hearing the "C" word in a doctor's office. Grief comes into our lives through many avenues, each one bringing grief that takes on a little different twist.

The grief of having a child with Same-Sex Attraction is one of those. The child you carried in your own body, the child you gave birth to, taught to walk, talk and play well with others has become someone you barely recognize. You thought you knew this child. She gave her life to Christ at a young age. She grew up going to church and had good Christian friends. She volunteered one summer at an inner-city mission, feeding the homeless and caring for the poverty-stricken.

Then she "came out."

She walked away from God, from everything you taught her, and from every dream you ever held for her. Now she's in a homosexual relationship.

Some will tell you it's not the end of the world. They're right; it's not the end of the world, but it is the end of a lot of things. It's the end of the child you knew—or thought you knew. It may seem as though another person has taken his place; someone who is bitter and hateful and mean, or someone who is crude and vulgar and harsh. Perhaps if you're fortunate, you still see the person your child always was, just with a different lifestyle and different perspectives on some issues. Whatever the case, his journey into a homosexual lifestyle is the end of certain hopes and dreams. Yes, very often it feels like a death, only there is no funeral, no flowers, and no memorial service for the person you once knew.

Our culture will tell you homosexuality is not even a big deal. *"It's just love, and love is good!"* To a Bible-believing Christian, one who knows God's Word and His heart, no, homosexuality is not good. It's painful. It's a whole bunch of losses. Barbara Johnson said it well: *it's agony.*

At first the shock is…profound. A numbness settles in for many of us. Then one day the numbness goes away and grief comes crashing in like a tsunami. It knocks you off your feet. You feel like you can't breathe. You don't even recognize the voice wailing in your ears, until you realize it's you who's doing the wailing. It's your voice, but it's a voice that has been altered by grief.

As time goes by, life goes on and the grief begins to subside. It still comes crashing in at times, but the waves get smaller in size and strength. Eventually they stop knocking you down, and instead of torrents of tears that feel like they will never cease, you cry hard for a few moments, wipe your eyes, and go on with your day.

If you're fortunate, you have someone with whom to share your grief—someone who feels that grief too—or at least someone who understands it. Pity the person who endures this grief alone. I'm not sure anyone can survive such grief alone.

Hopefully, during even these early days of grief, you are able to keep it together around your son or daughter. You watch what you say, how you react to things he says. You smile and laugh with her as though everything is fine. Of course, it's not fine and it may never be fine again.

You learn to cope. You learn to accept the situation for what it is. Maybe you even learn to appreciate the good things in your child's life in spite of the losses.

One thing is certain: this is a grief that we, as parents, were never meant to bear.

The Grief Cycle

You may be familiar with the stages of grief outlined in numerous psychology books and counseling manuals, however the grief cycle[7] for parents of adult kids with SSA can look different.

When the initial loss hits you, you may feel like you're talking to a stranger when speaking with your child. You may feel betrayed or insecure in your relationship with him or her. In fact, the core of your relationship with she is forever changed; a shift has occurred. The relationship is still there, but it feels like it will never be as it was before. Perhaps it will be better, or it may be worse. Know, however, that it has indeed changed. You may begin to second-guess yourself, or to question her, or to repeatedly go over things from the past. You may feel a deep sense of loss when looking through pictures from her childhood.

During the time of the initial loss you may feel that things are spinning out of control, causing feelings of helplessness or panic to arise. You may experience the loss of your dreams for your child—that perfect wedding or having grandchildren someday, for example. You may fear the loss of your reputation, especially if you are active in church service. You may fear rejection from friends, family, or your church. This fear may leave you feeling isolated, alone, and condemned.

Following the initial loss, the **first stage** of grief is one of shock. This time may be marked by feeling your life has been wrecked, shattered, or devastated. Excessive crying interspersed with feelings of numbness or feeling dead inside is common for women. You may also experience physical symptoms such as a loss of appetite, unexplained nausea, migraine headaches, difficulty sleeping, exhaustion, disinterest in marital intimacy, or depression.

Men tend to go into denial at this stage, while women often experience the more intense emotions. The father may say things like, "Oh, he is young, this is just a phase," or "She's just in rebellion. She'll get over this." These fathers are responding with denial, which is a form of self-protection and is a natural coping mechanism *for a time*. For these fathers, this is their safe place to go in a situation that is beyond their ability to deal, initially. If you are married to one of these men, or if you are that man, employ grace instead of judgment. Allow each other, as parents of the child, to process this new life situation in whatever way is most natural and beneficial at this stage of the grief cycle. Be kind to one another, and do not place your expectations or emotions on the other person.

These responses are typical in this set of circumstances, but if you are experiencing something else, that's okay too. These are typical responses, not hard and fast rules of how to respond.

Go *with* the process. For example, when you can't sleep, read your Bible. Look for verses of hope and of God's heart for you and your child. Journal. Talk through your feelings with someone. If you don't feel anything, know this numbness is temporary. You're in a stage of shock in the same way the body goes into shock after a serious physical injury. Your emotions are in a stage of shock. At some point the numbness will wear off.

The **second stage** of this type of grief is one of protest. It's an intense turmoil with extremely intense emotions. *Don't stuff your feelings! Instead, press into the pain.* Give yourself permission to release the emotions you're feeling, through crying, yelling, screaming—whatever feels natural to you. Pain that we deny or fight will find other ways to come out. While no one enjoys pain or looks forward to it, pain is a normal part of this process. The most beneficial way of dealing with it is to look it square in the face, feel it, and release it. You can't release what you haven't embraced. It's okay; you may feel as though you will lose yourself or possibly your mind, but you won't. *You will get through this.*

It is normal at this stage to feel deep sorrow. This pain may increase as you see other families experiencing the "normal" things of life, such as a daughter marrying her longtime boyfriend, or a son and his wife who are expecting their first child. Remember that *comparison is the enemy of peace and joy.* Be happy for those who are enjoying such wonderful times in their families, but give yourself permission to grieve privately.

You may experience anger in any form: rage, explosive anger, irritability, seething anger, or buried anger, which may present itself as depression. You may feel panicked about the future, about how others will react to you or to your child. You may experience feelings of fear over the depression or suicidal tendencies he may face, or the potential for diseases such as AIDS. You may feel a desperate need to find answers or solutions—anything that will fix the current situation and make it all go away.

In this stage, more than any of the others, you may be tempted to rail at God. During this time, especially, it's important to realize that *God is not the enemy.* It is normal and common to ask God, "Why?" and to do so with a degree of anger and resentment. Recognize He understands your heart and your emotions better than you do. When you are hurting, He's hurting right along with you, much the same as we hurt when our kids hurt. However, it is important to resist the temptation to accuse God, to blame Him, or to turn your back on Him. He did not bring this upon your child, but He can bring him out of it. There are no guarantees He will, but God is the only hope your son has of ever being set free from SSA or the homosexual lifestyle. Partner with Him through prayer, love, surrender, and obedience. Allow Him to lead you. He will not lead you astray.

Take notice of emotional triggers in this stage. Whenever something sets you off (causing feelings of anger, angry outbursts, irritability, sadness, etc.), make a mental note of that so it won't catch you off guard in the future. You won't be able to stave off every trigger, but the more you take notice of what stirs your emotions, the less frequently you will be blindsided.

The **third stage** of this grief cycle is a time of seeming chaos. You may feel as though you've lost your footing. Things that used to be normal parts of your routine may feel awkward and foreign. You may find yourself shutting down, isolating, or losing interest in things you used to enjoy. At times, you may yearn for the way things were before your child came out. The longing that comes during this stage can be especially difficult. You may even be unable, at times, to get her SSA off your mind. It's not uncommon to focus obsessively on the situation for a time. However, if it becomes a pattern, or you feel unable to stop thinking about it constantly, it may be time to seek out professional help. (See the guides it the Appendix.)

If your child has publicly come out, you may fear the reactions or responses of other people, causing you to avoid situations where people may ask about your son or daughter. You may be feeling shame or embarrassment, while others may have celebrated and applauded his coming out. In our current cultural climate, it's important to note that there will always be some people who will encourage your son's homosexuality or say hurtful things. Some will do so because they like to stir the pot; others will do so out of wanting to say the right thing and simply not knowing what that is. In a later chapter, we will discuss how to deal with these situations. But for now, simply know that while your feelings are valid, hiding away is never the answer. Foregoing a social event now and then as a means of self-care is not a problem, but if you realize you are isolating too frequently or for unhealthy reasons, it's time to re-evaluate.

This brings us to another similar topic: getting stuck and resisting moving on. In this stage of chaos, it may feel better to try to bury yourself in busywork or to isolate as previously discussed. The reality is your child's current sexual identity is your new reality, unless or until such a time when God begins to change her heart. While He can do this at any time, it could feasibly be decades before your daughter's heart begins to heal. In the meantime, our job as parents is to keep moving forward, to embrace the way things are in a healthy manner, and to accept the situation for what it is at this point in time. *We must never give up hope that our children will be set free from SSA, but we must get on with the business of living in the reality of the moment.* If you want to have a good relationship with your SSA child, moving on with your life and accepting things as they are (without condoning his or her sinful behavior) is necessary for your bond to remain strong.

In this stage, as in the first two, it is vital to be intentional about taking care of yourself: body, soul, and spirit. Take time to process things, but don't obsess. Take time to rest and relax, but don't quit life. Balance is the key word here. Make time for being with people you can trust to listen when you need to talk, and to distract you with fun or entertainment, etc. when you need to get out of your head. Strive for balance, authenticity, and honesty within the context of a caring community. (We will discuss self-care more thoroughly in Chapter 7.)

The **fourth stage** of the grief cycle is a time of reorganization. It emerges when things begin to become routine again. The overwhelming grief has been replaced by occasional sadness. You may even find yourself discovering hope again, along with a return to spiritual growth and purpose. This stage is marked by a new level of acceptance, learning to let go of what you can't control, and moving beyond the confines of grief and loss. Accept reality, but hold onto hope in Jesus. It is a time to accept and step into all the responsibilities you may have let fall by the wayside. This stage is marked by waking up, getting up, and moving forward beyond the deep grief and extreme emotions. Realize however, that you can't force this stage, but you can be intentional about dealing with your emotions, identifying the triggers that set you off, and taking good care of yourself. As you do those things, little by little the deep sadness, obsessive thoughts, and intense emotions will begin to subside. (If they don't, you may need to seek professional help.) Life will feel more normal again. It might not be the normal you used to have, but the new normal of being the parent of a child with SSA.

This grief process is not linear. You may go back and forth through various stages from one week to the next, or one minute to the next. Be patient with yourself and with your spouse. Trust God in this process, and remember He is with you every step of the way. There is nowhere on this planet you can go where His Spirit is not with you (Psalm 139). He will never leave you nor forsake you, especially in a time of deep grief (Deuteronomy 31:8). Be aware God is changing you through this pain and grief. God uses the painful things in this life to transform us into His image, and that is a good thing (2 Corinthians 3:18)! Remember also He has plans and purposes for us, plans to bless us and not to harm us, to give us hope and a future; and when we seek Him with our whole heart we will find Him because He is always right there with us (Jeremiah 29:11-12). If, however, you find that you are stuck in any part of this process, there are things you can do to get unstuck.

Getting Unstuck

When you realize you're stuck in any of the first three stages of the grief cycle, there are some specific steps you can take to get unstuck. Everything starts with awareness. Once you know you are in a rut—or a destructive cycle—assess, admit, and ask.

- Assess where you are stuck (which phase)
- Admit you need help
- Ask for help
  - Get a physical exam if needed
  - Establish a support system
  - Get into counseling
  - Consider talking with your doctor about obtaining anti-depressants

As I said earlier, you don't have to go through this alone. In fact, I highly recommend you don't even try. There is always help available, but it won't come to you. This SSA may be your child's issue, but it changes major aspects of your life and therefore has a deep impact on you. While you can't change your son or his situation, you have a responsibility to take proper care of yourself. You may have to go outside your comfort zone. It's not always easy to ask for help, but you can do it. If you are stuck in an unhealthy place within the grief cycle, you must!

NOTE: It's important to note that this lesson was written with parents of *adult* children with SSA in mind. If your child is a minor, your acceptance of the situation "as it is" will look different. As the parent of a minor child living with you, you have a responsibility to intervene in her life in order to help her to deal with her SSA feelings before acting upon them, if possible. This intervention may include heart-to-heart discussions between you and your daughter, family and individual therapy, counseling, or professional coaching, and boundaries and limits to safeguard her. It is recommended that, at the very least, you speak with a qualified, caring mental health professional about how to intervene on behalf of your minor child in an effective and healthy manner. (See the related articles in the Appendix for more information.) Few if any children will be happy about the realization that they have Same-Sex Attraction. As the parent of these children, you have a unique opportunity to empower them to not go down that path. Again, you cannot control your son or change his Same-Sex Attraction, but you can provide resources and help that may rescue him <u>before</u> he fully accepts a homosexual identity and begins to live the homosexual lifestyle.

DIGGING DEEPER: Journal Questions

1. Which of the phases of the grief cycle can you relate to? Explain.

2. Have you experienced moving back and forth through the cycles? Which ones?

3. Which phase are you in now? Explain.

4. Do you feel stuck in any one stage? If so, which one?

5. Do you need to ask for help to get unstuck? If so, write out a commitment to yourself of what your plan of action will be in obtaining that help. Acknowledge God in this process, and commit this plan to Him as well.

6. If you are married, how is your spouse responding to the issue? Is your relationship with your spouse suffering because of grief (either yours or your spouses), or is it becoming stronger? Are you able to talk about your grief with each other? Assess your expectations and seek counseling or coaching if you are struggling in your marriage.

7. Write out Deuteronomy 31:8 in your journal. Where does this verse say that God is in your time of need? What is His promise to you? Do you believe what this verse says? Why or why not?

8. What effect does Deuteronomy 31:8 have on your fears or discouragement?

9. Write out a brief prayer to God about what you're feeling right now in regard to this week's lesson. (Be completely honest with Him; He knows anyway!)

DEEPER STILL: Study Questions

1. Can you relate to the Barbara Johnson quote at the beginning of this lesson? Can you relate to the word *agony*? Why or why not? What words would you use to describe how your child's SSA has made you feel?

2. Read Psalm 139:7-10. What do these verses say about where God is in our times of pain and suffering?

3. Do those verses in Psalm 139 bring you comfort? Why or why not?

4. Read 1 Kings 19:1-18 and answer the following questions.

   a. What was Elijah feeling in verses 3 and 4?

   b. What did he pray for?

   c. What did God do for Elijah in verses 5-7?

   d. Was God's response to Elijah harsh and uncaring, or compassionate and understanding?

   e. In verse 10, Elijah complained to God about his circumstances. Verse 11 says that there was a powerful wind, an earthquake, and a fire, but God was not in those. Instead, what came after the fire? What does that mean to you in your time of grief?

   f. In verse 14, Elijah repeats his complaint. Was there more to the story than Elijah realized? Did that make a difference to what Elijah was feeling? Explain.

   g. Have you ever felt like Elijah did in verse 4, that you "have had enough?"

h. Read Psalm 34:18. Do you think God understands how you're feeling and that He is compassionate toward you? Why or why not?

i. Have you looked at the painful circumstances of your child's SSA and somehow believed God was causing them? We often believe God is in the "damaging wind, earthquakes, and fires" that threaten our peace, joy, and even our lives. In doing so, we accuse Him of being hurtful or mean. But consider for a moment He's not in those things, but instead, He is responding to your heartache and fears with a gentle whisper, and with a desire to meet your needs…. Take a few moments to sit quietly before the Lord and ask Him to speak to your heart. If you sense Him saying anything to you, write it down here.

j. Is it possible there is more to your story with your SSA child than you know? Is it possible God is working in your child's story even though you don't see it for yourself?

APPLICATION: Write out your takeaway.

_____

_____

_____

_____

_____

GROUP SESSION:
Chapter Four
The Path of Grief

*"The LORD is close to the brokenhearted and saves
those who are crushed in spirit."*

Psalm 34:18

ഇൽ

*"Finding out about a gay child is agony.
It's almost like having a death in the family.
But when someone dies you can bury
that person and move on with your life.
With homosexuality, the pain seems never-ending."*

Barbara Johnson, *Where Does A Mother Go to Resign?*[8]

No one likes to grieve, but sometimes there is simply no other response to a situation. The word *agony* is indeed a powerful one. It is a word that exemplifies this grief.

Agony is defined as, "great pain or anguish; intense emotion."

Has it ever occurred to you, in light of the discussion in our country, how something our culture sees as good, is actually causing so much agony? And what of the agony our children felt when they first realized they were experiencing Same-Sex Attraction? If homosexuality is such a good thing, why is the suicide rate for these kids six times higher than that of heterosexual kids?[9] Is it really as simple as changing our perspective about it?

Our society can call it good, but as Rick Warren (Saddleback Church) said, *"A lie doesn't become truth, wrong doesn't become right, and evil doesn't become good just because it's accepted by a majority."*[10] Now, I don't believe a majority of people in our country have accepted SSA as "true, right or good," but the LGBT community has certainly made tremendous headway in this area, and in a relatively short amount of time. However, does it matter what our society says? Our own hearts and the hearts of our children have testified to the contrary—which, not coincidentally, is right in line with God's Word concerning homosexuality.

Maybe your SSA child is older and has been "out" for decades. Maybe she has found a long-term partner which whom to share her life. Perhaps they seem to be a very happy and well-adjusted couple. Does that change the reality of the situation from God's perspective, or from the perspective of a grieving parent? Does their 'happiness' somehow erase the years of agony? What about that? What does their current situation of apparent happiness say to those of us whose hearts are in agony for our children?

Your adult child may seem happy and well-adjusted in his homosexual partnership while the person sitting next to you may have an adult SSA child who is addicted to drugs because of his SSA. The guy next to you may have a daughter who self-harms because of her SSA. The woman across the room may have lost a child to suicide because of his SSA. Another person's child may have AIDS because of his homosexual behavior. *Do the circumstances of a situation determine if something is right or wrong, good or bad?* No! Certainly not! That is why we need the definitive Word of God to shape our perspectives. God is not a God of situational ethics. He is the one and only—and final—arbiter of what is right and good and beneficial.

The topic of Same-Sex Attraction is one of great pain, anguish, and intense emotions that causes much grief on many fronts. Our pain and anguish is legitimate. It is valid. No society or culture can shame us or name-call us or bully us out of feeling what we feel, or out of believing anything contrary to God's Word and character. It is extremely disrespectful for them to even consider doing so. Our feelings are no more or less valid than anyone else's.

Discussion questions:

1. Why does the SSA of our children cause such grief?

2. Can you relate to the word, "agony," in regard to your child's SSA? Why or why not?

3. Which of the phases of the grief cycle can you relate to? Explain.

4. Have you experienced moving back and forth through the cycles? Which ones?

5. Which phase are you in now? Do you feel stuck in any one stage? If so, which one?

6. Do you need to ask for help to get unstuck?

7. If you are married, how is grief (yours or your spouse's) affecting your relationship with each other?

8. What did the story of Elijah in 1 Kings reveal to you about God's heart toward Elijah? Toward you?

9. What parts of that story stood out in your mind?

10. How does it feel when you hear someone talk about how wonderful it is to be 'gay'? Do you respond to them? What do you do with those feelings?

11. Can anyone else's perspective of SSA change, undo, or diminish your grief? Why or why not?

12. What questions from the lesson were most meaningful to you?

13. Your takeaway: If you were to sum up the impact of this week's lesson in one concise thought, what would that be?

14. Do you have any prayer requests pertaining to your child's SSA you would like to share?

Closing Prayer

Father God,

Our hearts are broken for our children, for our family, and because of the lost dreams we had for them. We surrender those lost dreams to You, Abba, along with all our other feelings of grief, anger, fear, and sadness. We offer these to You as a sacrifice of suffering; as a joining with the sufferings of Christ. May they be a sweet fragrance to You. Lord, we pray You will heal all our hearts—replacing the broken, hurting places with scars that remind us that You are faithful even when life hurts. May our scars be trophies of Your mercy and faithfulness toward us that we can show to others along this and other difficult paths. Use our pain for Your glory, and replace it with Your strength and a multiplied measure of faith as we continue in this fight. Thank You for walking with us every step of the way!

In the Mighty Name of Jesus,

Amen.

Chapter Five

FIGHTING THE GOOD FIGHT FOR YOUR CHILD

*"I looked for someone among them who would build
up the wall and stand before Me in the gap on behalf
of the land so I would not have to destroy it, but I
found no one."*

Ezekiel 22:30

ෂoෙ

*"...somehow we have overlooked the fact this treasure called
the heart can also be broken, has been broken, and now lies
in pieces down under the surface. When it comes to habits
we cannot quit or patterns we cannot stop, anger that flies
out of nowhere, fears we cannot overcome, or weaknesses
we hate to admit—much of what troubles us comes out of the
broken places in our hearts crying out for relief."*

John Eldredge, *Waking the Dead: The Glory of a Heart Fully Alive*[11]

As a little girl, she had the biggest, most expressive eyes. As sweet as warm honey on a hot summer's day, this little girl was pure delight. She had the kindest heart, one filled with compassion for those around her. Anytime anyone in the house was sick, this little girl would, at some point, present the ailing person with some token of love—a picture she had drawn or a rose she had fashioned out of construction paper, or a favorite stuffed animal on loan to provide comfort.

She was painfully shy around strangers, but in the company of family and close friends, this girl had an infectious sense of humor. She was sharp and witty, often surprising in the hilarity she brought to just about any situation. She was such a joy.

However, there was another side to this sweet child. She had endured some fairly daunting heart wounds in her short life: hardships no child should have to face. But face them she did. Sometimes she would go on as if nothing was different about her life. Other times she would reveal a steely determination. Her strength of will showed through at these times. This girl was a force to be reckoned with!

Both tender and tough, compassionate and determined, this child lit up every room she entered. She was walking sunshine, bright and cheery, or when she reached her limit, as scorching as a summer heatwave. On the rare occasion, the cracks in her otherwise steely armor would reveal the wounded heart beneath. The most sensitive hearts are the ones most vulnerable to being wounded.

I imagine the narrative above could describe many of the children this book represents. They are sensitive, compassionate, intelligent, and creative children; children who have endured deep cuts to the soft flesh of their sensitive hearts. They have been appallingly wounded.

Because of their sensitivity, they were especially vulnerable to critical comments, harsh words, put-downs, or rejections in any form. They were especially vulnerable to those with unkind hearts. For many of these kids, they developed anxiety issues with equally effective strategies for hiding their pain and unease. What we as parents saw as impatience or irritability may have been full-blown anxiety.

This perspective is that of a mom in hindsight, but it is still seriously lacking. What is missing? It's missing awareness of the unseen battle, the war that was raging against that child. John Eldredge says there are three truths about this world we must know. The first is that we have a very real enemy. Second is that we are at war with that enemy. Third is that we have a job to do. Our job is to recognize the war raging against those we love and us, and to do battle with our enemy.

Scripture says our enemy is His enemy, first and foremost. Therefore, when we belong to God, he becomes our enemy as well. Scripture refers to him by many names: the deceiver (2 John 7), the father of lies (John 8:44), the accuser (Revelation 12:10), the serpent (Genesis 3:1-4), the devil (1 John 3:8, 1 Peter 5:8), Satan (2 Corinthians 2:10-12), a fallen angel (Isaiah 14:12-15), an angel of light (2 Corinthians 11:14), the tempter (Matthew 4:3) the evil one (Matthew 13:38-40), and the antichrist (1 John 4:3). His number one priority is to undermine God in any way he can, and all the better if he can distract, discourage, or destroy the hearts and lives of those in God's family. According to Scripture, he has come to steal our joy, our true identity, our faith, hope, and love, to kill our hearts, to destroy us from the inside out (John 10:10), to deceive us (2 John 7), confuse us, tempt us to sin (Genesis 3), and to accuse the children of God (Revelation 12:10). Scripture says it very clearly:

> *For our struggle is not against flesh and blood, but against the rulers, against the authorities, against the powers of this dark world and against the spiritual forces of evil in the heavenly realms."*
>
> Ephesians 6:12

Satan is the leader of those "spiritual forces of evil," and he's really good at what he does.

He knows us better than we know ourselves, and he and his cadre have been working against us since our earliest childhood, planting seeds of unworthiness, heartbreak, and insufficiency in our hearts and minds. For our children with such sensitive hearts, his attacks were laser-focused on destroying their healthy attachment and sense of belonging with others of their gender. For some, this occurred through rejection, a feeling of being different, teasing, put-downs, or criticism. For others, the conduit was emotional, physical, sexual, or verbal abuse by those who were more powerful than them. (Refer back to Chapter 2 to review the complete list of factors contributing to SSA.)

What are we, their parents, to do in response?

First, let's talk about what *not* to do. Remember your child is not the enemy! Do not judge, condemn, preach at, or reject your son—

ever—and especially not with the hopes of changing him. *We cannot change another person*. The only person we can change is the one staring back at us from the mirror. Judging, condemning, preaching at, or lecturing your son will only push him away. Therefore, do not lecture him, shame him, or tell him what a disappointment he has become to you. Do not harp on your daughter constantly about her choices, her failures, or her appearance. No one responds well to these kinds of verbal lashings. Remember: these have *sensitive hearts* that are especially prone to pick up on, internalize, and respond strongly to negative experiences. Whatever negative comment we say to them is amplified within their sensitive hearts, and may reverberate relentlessly within their minds.

What we *can* do is to love them where they are, with unconditional love and acceptance (without approving of wrong behavior), and *fight for them*. What does that fighting look like? Do they even need to know we are fighting for them?

Fighting the good fight for our kids is primarily about two things. It is about standing in the gap for them where God is concerned, and it is about fighting the enemy of their souls. (And no, there is no reason to tell them you are doing battle for them.) Let's take a brief look at each of those.

Standing in the Gap

When our kids are "off the rails" in their life situations or decisions, when they have turned their backs on God, or when they are pursuing God while still living a homosexual lifestyle, there is a gap in their spiritual life. Wholeheartedly living for God is choosing to live in a manner that is pleasing to Him. It's not living a life without sin; that's quite impossible. But it is living without *intentional* sin, to the best of our ability and with the enabling of the Holy Spirit. Choosing to live a homosexual lifestyle is intentionally choosing to sin. I'm not talking about temptation here, but about crossing over from temptation to action.

That choice to enter into sinful behavior intentionally is where the gap is. It can be a gap the size of the Grand Canyon, or it may be small enough to step across, but it is still a gap. It reminds me of taking the trains in Europe, and the constant reminders to "Mind the Gap!" Gaps are dangerous places. Sometimes they are even deadly.

What does it mean to "stand in the gap" for someone? Very simply, it is standing in for them in this area of their relationship with God until they are willing or able to do so. It is a stand we take on our knees, in prayer, in praise, in truth, and in trust.

Prayer is the first order of business, and it is the most powerful weapon we possess. It is taking our requests and the desires of our heart to God based on the *truth* of who He is, His promises to us, and our identity as children of the Most High God. First and foremost, we must pray according to what is true. That truth is that your child's identity is sealed in Jesus Christ, the God of her salvation; it is not defined by Same-Sex Attraction or by living the homosexual lifestyle in which she may currently be engaging. Truth is the basis for all of our prayers and praises, our thoughts, our desires, and our hope. We all struggle with sin, but our identity is not defined by our struggles. It is defined by who Jesus says we are. Pray for her to surrender her heart to Him, and to accept who He says she is.

Praise is the second weapon we wield as we stand in the gap for our children. The hardest time to praise God is when everything seems hopeless, when our hearts are broken, and when we feel like doing anything *but* giving Him praise. Because praising God in the midst of a trial is so difficult, it becomes a *sacrifice* of praise (Hebrews 13:15). When we can summon the strength to praise Him in the midst of our personal storms and chaos, something within us shifts. It's as though somewhere a relief valve has been opened, and as we offer Him our praise-soaked pain, our hearts become lighter. By His Spirit He enters into our praises and our pain in a special way (Psalm 22:3). The King James Version of the Bible uses the word *inhabits*, saying, in effect, that He inhabits the praises of His people. Further, the enemy cannot tolerate being in the presence of praise to God. The result is that, as we praise, he will flee! Prayer is the first vital weapon in our arsenal. Praise is the second.

Finally, the third aspect of spiritual warfare is *trust*. Trust is standing firm in the faith that God is who He says is, that He is able to do what He says He will do. It is faith in His promises to us and to our children. It is believing that He hears us when we pray, He cares about the situation at hand, and He is already working on behalf of our children and us. In short, it is entrusting our cares to Him because we know and believe He cares for us (I Peter 5:7).

In this process, we are asking God—through prayer and praise, according to His truth, and with sincere faith and trust in Him—to work in our child's heart, mind, body, soul, spirit, and circumstances to deliver, transform, and to restore him to the person He called and created him to be. Ask God to heal the wounded places in the heart of your child, to renew her mind, to give her the mind of Christ, and a desire for righteousness. Ask Him to bring these kids to the end of themselves and for them to find Jesus there, arms open wide, waiting for them when they do. It is praying for them, asking for God's mercy and protection for them, and it is asking Him to forgive them. For truly, in the area of SSA behavior, they "know not what they are doing" (Luke 23:34). Oh sure, they know on some level; but if they *really* knew what they were doing, they wouldn't be doing it. That's where prayer for them to return to their senses comes in! Ask God to replace the lies and deceptions of the enemy with His truth; to soften their hearts toward Christ, and to purify them, body, soul, mind, and spirit. Ask Him to take what the enemy meant for evil in their lives and to use it for good. Ask Him to give them the desire for transformation, and the motivation to pursue Christ with their whole hearts. Ask Him to give you His wisdom, discernment, and clarity in every interaction with them. Ask Him to speak through you by His Spirit, for His glory and purposes, and to put a guard over your mouth when necessary (Psalm 141:3). Ask Him to take back that which belongs to Him. If they have previously given their lives to Christ, they belong completely to Him. The enemy has no claim on their lives. If they haven't surrendered their lives to Christ, ask Him to awaken their spirit to their need for a Savior, and for them to know that Savior is Jesus Christ.

Pray for their current relationship if they are in one, that God will change their hearts toward each other, draining away any attraction, bond, addiction, or dependence that may exist between them. Ask

Him to move in the heart, mind, and spirit of their partner, healing her heart wounds as well. Ask Him to break every lie, deception, or stronghold of the enemy that is keeping them captive to their sin, and thank Him in advance for the day when they both are truly free from the sin of homosexuality.

In short, praying for them in this manner is standing in the gap in their lives until such time as they are able to do so.

Fighting the Enemy of Their Souls

The other side of this coin is doing battle for your child against the enemy. Pray for the weapons and schemes of the enemy to fail in every attempt, that no weapon formed against them would be successful because this is his heritage in the family of God.

> *"...no weapon forged against you will prevail,*
> *and you will refute every tongue that accuses you.*
> *This is the heritage of the servants of the LORD,*
> *and this is their vindication from Me,'*
> *declares the LORD."*
> Isaiah 54:17

Ask God to remember His promises for your child as laid out in Scripture. Ask Him to tear down every stronghold and to return to the enemy what he intended for your son or daughter, a thousand-fold.

Speak God's truth aloud to the enemy, as you feel led to do so. Following are some guidelines:

- It is written that the Lord said, *"I have summoned [child's name] by name; you are [she is] Mine" (Isaiah 43:1b).* Therefore, [child's name] does not belong to you, Satan; you have no authority or claim to her life.

- It is written that the Lord Jesus said, *"I give (gave) [child's name] eternal life, and [she] shall never perish; no one will snatch [her] out of my hand. My Father, who has given [her] to me, is greater than all; no one can snatch [her] out of* my Father's hand. *I and the Father are one" [John 10:28-30]*. Therefore Satan, you have no claim to [child's name]; not even you can snatch him/her from God's hand. For this reason, you must submit to the Most High God and release this child from all influence from your lies, deceptions, strongholds, etc. in Jesus' Name and by His blood shed on the cross for [child's name]'s sin.

- It is written that the Lord Jesus said, *"And this is the will of Him who sent Me, that* I shall lose none of all those He has given me, *but raise them up at the last day" (John 6:39)*. Therefore, this child will not be forever lost in your web of lies and deceit. Nothing you can do will change who he is in Christ. In the Name of Jesus and by His blood, you are commanded to flee and never return to [child's name].

- It is written that, *"the one who is in you [child's name] is greater than the one who is in the world" (1 John 4:4)*. Therefore, because the Holy Spirit lives within this child, you must relinquish [child's name] to the Most High God. You have no power over him/her.

- It is written, *"Then Jesus came to them and said, "All authority in heaven and on earth has been given to Me" (Matthew 28:28)*. Therefore, you have no authority over [child's name]. You must submit to the authority of Jesus, in His Name, by His blood shed on behalf of [child's name].

- It is written, *"...neither death nor life, neither angels nor demons, neither the present nor the future, nor any powers, neither height nor depth, nor anything else in all creation, will be able to separate [child's name] from the love of God that is in Christ Jesus our Lord" (Romans 8:38-39)*. Therefore, because the love and Spirit of God have sealed [child's name] in Christ Jesus, you must release this child from any and all claims, influences, schemes, or designs you have placed upon him/her.

- It is written, *"Submit yourselves, then, to God. Resist the devil, and he will flee from you" (James 4:7)*. Therefore, because [child's name] has previously submitted herself to God, becoming a child of the Most High God, and as her parent and also a Child of the Most High God, and on her behalf, I command you to release her and go directly to the throne of God where you must do as He says.

- It is written, *"And the devil, who deceived them, was thrown into the lake of burning sulfur, where the beast and the false prophet had been thrown. They will be tormented day and night for ever and ever"* Revelation 20:10. This is your future, Satan! You will pay for all eternity for what you have done to the Beloved Bride of Christ! And it is in His Name that I, a Son/Daughter of the Most High God, command you to flee and never return!

Standing in the gap for a child in bondage to homosexuality is not for the faint of heart or the frail of faith! You must "clean your own house" before God, prior to doing battle for your child. You must also be prepared for the enemy to strike back. He will not give up on him easily or quickly! A crucial part of your preparation for this fight is putting on the armor of God (see Ephesians 6:10-18). Without wearing this armor daily, we run the risk of getting knocked down or knocked out. We cannot fight this enemy in our own strength. Our success rests on our ability to fight this fight in God's strength, by His Spirit, and with His provision—and a key part of that provision is the armor of God.

Standing in the gap may be a daily battle for a very long time. At times you will be tempted to give up. *Don't!* Never give up on your child! If you aren't doing battle for him in prayer, who will? This is a battle worth fighting. If you are faithful to the end, you will not regret one moment of standing in the gap or fighting for her.

DIGGING DEEPER: Journal Questions

1. Read the quote from John Eldredge at the top of this chapter. How does this quote relate to your child's SSA/behavior?

2. What are some of the areas of wounding you have identified in your son or daughter's heart? Go back and look at the 10 Factors that may lead to SSA from Chapter 2. Review those areas of wounding previously written in your journal.

3. Create a prayer list in your journal regarding these areas of wounding. Pray specifically for God to heal your child's heart in these areas and in any others that may have led him/her to SSA.

4. What areas of 'house-cleaning' do you need to do regarding your own walk with God? Do you have areas of intentional sin that you have been ignoring? Write those out in your journal and next to each one write whether or not you are willing to give up any and all intentional sins. If you are willing, give those things to God in prayer. If not, ask Him to make you willing to be willing. If there are areas in which you are unwilling to pray that prayer, write: "I am unwilling to give up this intentional sin."

5. Journal about why you are unwilling to give up that sin, as well as the price you are now paying or may someday pay for that sin. Be honest with yourself before God. He already knows everything in your heart. Ask Him to speak to your heart about that area of sin.

6. Does being honest with yourself about your own intentional sin help you relate better to where your child may currently be? How? Does that help you know better how to pray for him? For yourself?

DEEPER STILL: Study Questions

1. Read Luke 23: 26-37. What did Jesus pray in verse 34? Who was He praying for? Why do you think He prayed that prayer? How does this prayer apply to your child with SSA?

2. Where there is a wound, there is a need for healing. Write out what Jesus healed the people of in the following verses and anything notable about that event. Did He ever encounter anything He couldn't heal?

   a. Matthew 4:24

   b. Matthew 8:5-13

   c. Matthew 9:20-22

   d. Matthew 12:15

   e. Matthew 14:14

   f. Matthew 15:21-28

   g. John 11:38-44

   h. Luke 7:11-17

3. Standing in the gap for your son means praying *to* God and standing *against* the enemy based on the Word and power of God. Are you willing to stand in the gap for him? List the areas you need to specifically stand in the gap for him. (You may want to write these lists in your journal.)

Areas About Which to Pray to God	Areas in Which to Stand Against the Enemy

4. Read Ephesians 6:10-18. List the pieces of armor; discuss what each piece means and how it protects us from attacks of the enemy.

⇨ _____

⇨ _____

⇨ _____

⇨ _____

⇨ _____

⇨ _____

5. Read Hebrews 11, also known as the Hall of Faith. Standing in the gap for your child may be a very long process. Are you willing to stand in the gap for him/her for the long haul? Why or why not?

6. Hebrews 11:29-40 reveals a startling fact. What is that fact? Does your faith rest in the promise or in the promise Giver? What's the difference? Why is it important to make that distinction?

7. Because this journey into SSA may indeed be a long haul, what can you do to guard against discouragement or losing hope? Read Hebrews 12:1-3. What does this passage say about losing heart?

8. Why is it important to never lose hope that your child will be set free from the SSA lifestyle?

9. Of course, our desire is that our children will be delivered from homosexuality. However, it is possible that she may never come out of the homosexual lifestyle, or she may come out of the lifestyle, but never be set free from Same-Sex Attraction. It is possible that even without being delivered from SSA, she could go on to live a happy, satisfying, and fulfilling life—either remaining single and celibate, or entering into a heterosexual marriage and having a family. How do you feel about these possible outcomes? In an effort to "keep the main thing the main thing," what is the most important outcome for your child in all of these scenarios? (Colossians 1:10-11 holds the answer.)

10. If your child never leaves the homosexual lifestyle, what would your response likely be? Would you be tempted to accuse God of letting you and him down, of not hearing your prayers, not caring for you or your son, or of not keeping His promises, etc.? Read the following passages and identify the applicable truths therein:

a.   Isaiah 55:8-9

b.   Psalm 145:13b, 17-20

c.   Psalm 116:5

d.   Deuteronomy 32:4

11. Look up the definition of "righteous" in the Merriam-Webster Dictionary (online). What does it mean in regard to God? Can God do wrong or sin?

12. One definition of faith is, *"believing God even when everything around you speaks to the contrary."* Write out Hebrews 11:1 and, using these two references of faith, describe what faith means to you.

APPLICATION: Write out your takeaway.

_____

_____

_____

_____

_____

_____

_____

_____

_____

_____

_____

_____

_____

_____

_____

_____

_____

_____

Fighting the Good Fight for Your Child

"I looked for someone among them who would build
up the wall and stand before Me in the gap on behalf
of the land so I would not have to destroy it, but I
found no one."
Ezekiel 22:30

ℰℛ

"...somehow we have overlooked the fact this treasure called
the heart can also be broken, has been broken, and now lies
in pieces down under the surface. When it comes to habits
we cannot quit or patterns we cannot stop, anger that flies
out of nowhere, fears we cannot overcome, or weaknesses
we hate to admit—much of what troubles us comes out of the
broken places in our hearts crying out for relief."
John Eldredge, *Waking the Dead: The Glory of a Heart Fully Alive*[12]

Have you ever been in a real fight? Either a fistfight, a fight to be heard, or a fight for your life? Anyone who enters into any of these types of fights does so to win. No one enters a fight half-heartedly. The very word *fight* means you are ramped up. You are passionate about whatever the subject is, passionate enough to fight for it, and you are all in!

When you were faced with a child who came out, what was your natural instinct? Were you happy about the announcement? Were you sick to your stomach? Numb? Angry? Brokenhearted? Maybe you felt defeat or despair. Once the shock wore off, how did your feelings change? For many of us, we were ramped up, passionate about seeing our children set free from homosexuality, and passionate enough to fight for them.

The truth is, we <u>are</u> in a fight! We have a real enemy who has set his sights on our children, to deceive them, to destroy them and our family, and to divide us so he can conquer us. The truth is, in Christ, we are more than conquerors! However, it's not a victory that is handed to us on a silver platter. We have to be willing to fight this fight. We have to decide to be all in for the fight that is before us, and it's a fight in which we can never raise the white flag or throw in the towel. This is a fight for our kids, for our families, and for God's purposes. If ever there was a fight worth fighting, this is it!

Discussion questions:

1. What does it mean to stand in the gap for your child?

2. Are you willing and equipped to stand in the gap for your son or daughter for the long haul? Why or why not?

3. How does the John Eldredge quote relate to your son?

4. Where there is a wound, there is a need for healing. Do you believe God can heal your daughter?

5. What if that healing never takes place during your lifetime? What does that mean in your relationship with God?

6. Regarding Questions #8 and 9 in the Deeper Still section: What is the "main thing?" What is your hope—your deepest desire for your child? What if things don't go the way you would like for them to?

7. What do you believe God's deepest desire is for your son? For you, in this journey?

8. Did you learn anything new about yourself in this lesson? Are you willing to share that new awareness with the group?

9. Your takeaway: If you were to sum up the impact of this week's lesson in one concise thought, what would that be?

10. Do you have any prayer requests pertaining to your child's SSA you would like to share?

Closing Prayer

Father God,

Show us Your heart for our children. Direct our prayers for them as we commit to standing in the gap for them. Grow our faith to the measure of the difficulties, hardships, and hurts we face as parents of children with SSA that we may never lose heart or hope for the deliverance of our children from SSA/homosexual behavior. Heal their wounds, Father, and restore their identity in Christ Jesus to them. We know You love them even more than we do, that You have plans and purposes for their lives and ours, and that nothing is impossible with You. Help us to believe and to trust You regardless of the circumstances or the length of this journey.

In the Mighty Name of Jesus,

Amen.

Chapter Six

BEING CHRIST TO YOUR CHILD

*" I have been crucified with Christ and I no longer
live, but Christ lives in me.
The life I now live in the body, I live by faith in the
Son of God, who loved me and gave himself for me."*
Galatians 2:20

ഇൻഌ

"The one who loves best wins."
Richard Cohen, *Gay Children, Straight Parents: A Plan for Family Healing*[13]

She was a despised Samaritan woman. To her, He was a despicable Jew. The tension between them was set and ingrained by the culture of the day. Jews hated Samaritans, and the feeling was mutual. The midday sun was high and the heat was stifling, when this lone woman came to the well to draw water. The women of the town came to the well in the cooler hours of early morning or late evening, but not this woman. She came alone in the heat of the day to avoid the stares and comments and disdain. She was an outcast.

Weary from the day's travels, Jesus sat on the well to rest. It was there He broke protocol on so many levels! He, a man and a Jew, dared to speak to this Samaritan woman; a woman who came to the well when no one else would be there. Had the women of the town called her names? Had they turned their backs on her as they walked away whispering about her reputation? Jesus not only spoke to her, He asked her for water.

The woman was caustic in her responses to Jesus.

"Who are you to ask me for a drink," she asked, hatred dripping from her words.

"Who do you think you are? Do you think you're greater than our father Abraham?"

"Give me this 'living' water, so I never have to come to this well again...." Her sarcasm was biting; contempt for her station in life was clear.

When Jesus pulled back the curtain on the sinful and shameful circumstances of her life, like most of us would, she changed the subject. She deflected.

"Our ancestors worshiped here, but you Jews say we must worship in Jerusalem." She spat the words, "you Jews" at Jesus with more contempt, hoping to avoid the awkward and painful conversation concerning her sin.

After every caustic remark she made, however, Jesus, filled with nothing but love for this broken, wounded woman, replied to her with kindness and tenderness, giving her hope.

When she expected judgment and condemnation, Jesus gave her truth bathed in love. When she anticipated hatred and scorn, Jesus gave her kindness and hope and love.

The result was that the impossible happened that day. The transformation in this woman could not have been more startling. The outcast woman, who just moments before had dragged herself to the well in the noonday sun in order to avoid the townspeople, ran to where the people were, exclaiming with excitement that the Messiah had come! Not only had her life been changed, but Scripture says many Samaritans believed and came to meet Jesus as well.

ଚ୍ଚର

Let's face it; dealing with an issue as complex as Same-Sex Attraction and the homosexual behavior of our children is *hard*, and that's putting it mildly! From the moment our children came out to us, we have been bombarded with situations for which we were unprepared to deal. From that very first moment when our children revealed their secrets to us, expecting a caring, thoughtful, and supportive response right then and there, it has been a rollercoaster ride of ups and downs, twists and turns, and loop-the-loops. Being someone who never enjoyed crazy, theme park rides, I have to say I haven't been a fan of this rollercoaster either.

We want to respond to our children like Jesus responded to the Samaritan woman—with kindness, tenderness, and love—saying the right things. But left to our own devices—our flesh, as Scripture puts it—we are likely to mess up more often than we are to get it right. So what's a parent to do?

As Christians, we have the Holy Spirit within us. This third Person in the Trinity is always with us. Scripture describes Him as our Advocate, Counselor, and Comforter, the one who intercedes on our behalf and is always in tune with God the Father and Christ the Son (John 14:26; Philippians 2:1-2, Romans 8:26-27). He prays for us, guides us, and it is through Him that we experience the peace, comfort, and compassion of God, and the mind of Christ. With the Holy Spirit, we have a constant and abiding companion who is always available for whatever we need (Philippians 4:19).

So what *do* we need? We need more of Christ! Christ in us, working through us, giving to us what our kids need, and what *we* need. The difficulty is recognizing in that moment that we are in over our heads. Only then will we cry out to Him, *"I have no idea what to do or say here, but God, You do. You know what my child needs, and You alone can provide it."* That's the first step: awareness. The second is to pause to pray—right there in the moment—and ask Him to speak through you. That's what we need to do in order to be Christ to our kids no matter what they are going through.

What does it look like to "be Christ" to our kids who struggle with SSA? Let's take it one letter at a time.

C: "C" is for CHERISH your child. We need the love of Christ to fill us up in every situation we encounter with our SSA kids. When we are angry or hurt, when our children are behaving badly or hurtfully, we need His love to change our hearts, to help us to respond with lovingly instead of with anger or hurtful words of our own. When we are frustrated, discouraged, or simply don't feel like being kind or loving, or when he brings home a new partner, it is Christ's Spirit in us that enables us to cherish our son, to see past the sin and shame, and simply love him. Right then. Right there. In the moment. God's love is perfect; it casts out fear (I John 4:18), it ushers in compassion and every aspect of the fruit of the Spirit: love, joy, peace, patience, kindness, goodness, faithfulness, and self-control (Galatians 5:22-23). His uncommon love makes all the difference in how we love our kids.

H: "H" is for HONOR. Honor your child. When we disagree with their adult decisions, we can be tempted to show our disappointment, disapproval, or worse, try to manipulate them or guilt them into making a different decision. Those responses do not honor them. So how do we honor our children when they are making such bad decisions? We honor the honorable parts of the person we know them to be. For example, we can validate and affirm the good choices they make, or the kind, thoughtful, or loving gestures they exhibit. We can validate and affirm their work ethic or their integrity in other areas. However, these validations and affirmations must be authentic and honest. Our sensitive kids can smell a snow job or inauthenticity a mile away. This is why we need the Spirit to instruct us. Sometimes it can be hard to find those areas we sincerely honor and respect, especially when they are making such monumentally bad decisions and particularly in the areas associated with SSA. The Holy Spirit can and will guide us in honoring our children according to who He made them to be, authentically, sincerely.

R: The "R" in "CHRIST" is a reminder to RESIST the temptation to control, manipulate, condemn, judge, or show approval of sinful behavior. In order to be consistent in honoring our children, we must also resist the temptation to dishonor them. As adults, their choices are their own. As parents, we have done our part during their growing-up years to teach them how to make good decisions, to know right from wrong, and many other things. But that time is past. Now we have to let go of our adult children and allow them to rise or fall on their own merits—unless or until they ask for our opinions or help. But even at that point, we need to weigh our words carefully. Our kind and constructive (not destructive) criticism should be liberally sandwiched between the bread of encouragement, affirmation, validation, gentleness, and loving-kindness. Resist the urge to tear down. Build up by the Spirit instead.

I: "I" is for INTERCEDE. Intercession is simply praying on behalf of another. (Review this topic in the previous chapter if needed.) *Prayer according to the Holy Spirit will always be in line with God's Word and His will for your daughter.* Trust Him to lead you in the ways you need to pray for her. Ask Him daily, and every time she comes to mind, how you should pray for her. It doesn't have to be a lengthy prayer every time, but if He has brought her to mind, there's probably a reason. If she came to mind simply because you're worried about her, then that alone is a good reason to stop and pray. *Worry is a bully. It takes much and gives nothing of value in return.* Worry accomplishes nothing good, but the prayer of a faithful person is both powerful and effective, and it accomplishes much (James 5:16).

S: "S" is for SURRENDER. Surrendering your child to God is perhaps one of the most difficult things a parent is called to do. What does it mean to surrender your son to Him? It means taking your hands off, getting out of God's way, and leaving the circumstances and the outcomes in His capable hands. God loves him even more than you do, and He wants better for him than you do. And what's more, He knows *everything* there is to know about him. Nothing is hidden from God (Hebrews 4:13). He knows, He sees, and He cares, and He has plans and purposes for your son's life that you probably know nothing about. His plans are to prosper him, not harm him, which means you can trust God with your son's life (Jeremiah 29:11). Instead of trying to manage, manipulate, or manhandle your adult child with SSA, cherish him with the love of Christ, honor him in every way you honestly can, resist the temptation to judge or condemn him, and surrender him to the one who formed him in the secret places. (Psalm 139).

T: Finally, "T" is for TRUST. God is trustworthy. He is able. He is good. Even when all the circumstances you can see are bad or discouraging or hopeless, God never gives up on His children. If your child belongs to God, if God has spoken "Mine" over her, He has more of an investment in her than you do (Isaiah 43:1). In fact, she is more God's than she is yours. As His child, God is responsible for the life of your child in ways we cannot even imagine (Isaiah 48:11). Trust Him with her life. Trust Him today, and then trust Him again tomorrow, and purpose to trust Him again every day of her life. Doing so will enable peace to flood your soul, and His Spirit will sustain you (Isaiah 66:12).

Christ in you is the answer to all your hurts, fears, doubts, stress, and insufficiency. With His sufficiency, He can move mountains through us. He can raise the dead. He alone is the Healer, the Rebuilder, Restorer, and Redeemer (Isaiah 61:4). He alone can make beauty out of ashes (Isaiah 61:3). He alone can take what the enemy meant for evil and turn it into good (Genesis 50:20). Christ in you is the hope of glory (Colossians 1:27). Cherish and honor your child. Resist the temptation to judge, condemn, etc., and surrender her to God. Trust Him to do the impossible. It's what He does best!

DIGGING DEEPER: Journal Questions

1. What is your understanding of "being crucified with Christ?"

2. Write out each of the letters in the CHRIST acrostic and describe what that looks like for you in a practical sense, in relationship with your SSA child. Be specific.

3. Which of the words in the CHRIST acrostic are most challenging for you? Why?

4. In honoring your child, you must do so with honesty and authenticity. What challenges are you facing in that regard?

5. Do you see your child according to his identity as a homosexual, or as a child of the Most High God who is wounded, hurting, and struggling with sin? What difference does your view of your child make in your relationship with him?

6. Write your own prayer of surrender regarding your SSA child in your journal.

DEEPER STILL: Study Questions

1. What does the quote at the beginning of this chapter mean: *"The one who loves best wins?"*

2. Read Galatians 2:20. What did Jesus give up for you? Why did He do that?

3. Read 1 John 4:8. The word *love* here is the Greek word *agape, a form of the word agapao*. It is defined, according to Vine's Expository Dictionary, as: *"In respect of* agapao *as used of God, it expresses the deep and constant "love" and interest of a perfect Being towards entirely unworthy objects, producing and fostering a reverential "love" in them towards the Giver, and a practical "love" towards those who are partakers of the same, and a desire to help others to seek the Giver."* In short, agape love is defined by God, and indeed, He is the very core of it. Our culture, today insists that homosexual love is equal to God's love, that "it's just love, and love is good." What is the difference between God's agape love and homosexual love? Are they the same?

4. What is the warning in Isaiah 5:20? (According to the Gesenius' Hebrew-Chaldee Lexicon, the word *woe* in this verse is considered to be a threatening term.)

5. Read John 14:23-25. If we truly love God we will obey Him, which means putting Him first above all else. Putting God first means sometimes we have to sacrifice something we want in order to obey Him. What are you willing to sacrifice

to God out of love and obedience to Him? What, if anything, are you *unwilling* to sacrifice in order to obey God?

6. Read John 15:12. We are called to love one another as God loves us. How, then, do we love our children who are caught up in homosexual sin? Would Jesus compromise on the sin issue? Why or why not?

7. Read John 4:1-26. In a sentence or two, sum up how Jesus responded to this woman who was clearly living a life of sin. Did He compromise on or gloss over the issue of her sin?

8. In John 4:1-26, what two things did Jesus reveal are characteristic of the worshipers God seeks (verse 24)? Describe those two characteristics. Why are these characteristics important to God? How important should they be to us as Christians?

APPLICATION: Write out your takeaway.

_____

_____

_____

_____

_____

_____

GROUP SESSION:
Chapter Six

BEING CHRIST TO YOUR CHILD

*"I have been crucified with Christ and I no longer
live, but Christ lives in me.
The life I now live in the body, I live by faith in the
Son of God, who loved me and gave himself for me."*

Galatians 2:20

    ℰℭ

"The one who loves best wins."

Richard Cohen, *Gay Children, Straight Parents: A Plan for Family Healing*[14]

Love comes in many different forms. There is the love we have for a family member, and the love we have for ice cream! There's the love we have for a friend, and the love we have for our country, our home, and shopping great sales. (I love saving money. Don't you?) We throw the word *love* around pretty carelessly, don't we?

Scripture, itself, reveals at least three kinds of love: *agape, phileo,* and *eros. Agape* love is the deepest love; it is unconditional love that desires the best for the recipient—no matter what. *Agape* love sees beyond faults and flaws; it is sacrificial and expects nothing in return. It is the word that is used to describe God's love for us. *Phileo* is an affectionate, warm, and tender love as in a friendship. *Eros* is associated with romantic love, passion, and sexual love. *Eros* is more focused on self than on the other person.

It is important to understand the different types of love because *the one who loves best wins.* The love we have for our children is an undying, unconditional, sacrificial love. It is the love that expects nothing in return. No matter what our kids do, we love them the same. We may not like them very much at that moment. We may be hurt or offended by something they've said or done, but there is literally nothing in this world that can diminish the love we have had for our children since the first moment we held them in our arms. That is the love we have for them, and it is the love God has for us. This is important because God desires the very best for each and every one of us, and He will never, ever give up on us because He is the literal manifestation of *agape* love. His love is a love we can trust, and we can entrust our children to Him, loving them as He loves us. His love is the best love, and He will win. Our part is to receive His love, to live in obedience to Him, to get out of His way (by refusing to enable or rescue our children), and to let His love flow through us.

So how do we remain consistent in loving our wayward kids day-by-day, when we are worn out with worry, deeply grieved over their sin, or when their words or actions toward us are so hurtful? There is a *cycle of love* that makes this possible; it looks like this: God loves us unconditionally, to which our primary response should be to return that love to Him. As we love God in the ways He wants to be loved, through praising Him, revering Him, obeying Him, serving Him, and trusting Him (see Psalm 34:1-22), He gives us hope, comfort, peace, contentment, protection, and agape love without shame or condemnation. The psalmist sums it up with two simple words: *no lack.* Be aware, however, that although this process looks like a formula, it cannot be implemented as a formula. It requires that we enter into the process with our whole heart, authentically receiving His love, loving Him in return and being filled up with His provision that enables us to love our kids in the same way.

As we recognize and receive God's agape love for us, and we genuinely return that love to Him—loving Him in the ways He desires to be loved—He then fills us up with everything we need to pass that same love on to our kids. The result is that we have ample supply with which to love our kids unconditionally, no matter what. This is what it means to "love best."

Discussion questions:

1. What does it mean to "be crucified with Christ?"

2. In the CHRIST acrostic, which of these principles is the most challenging for you?

3. How are you doing with the tension between showing compassion to your SSA child without compromising your faith?

4. What does the quote, "The one who loves best wins" mean?

5. Is it possible to love badly or wrongly? What would that look like?

6. Is the "love cycle" referenced in the paragraphs above a "one and done" process? Why or why not?

7. God's Word says (in John 14:23-25) that if we love Him, we will obey Him. 1 Samuel 15:22 says it this way: "To obey is better than sacrifice…." Why is obedience to God so important?

8. What can we learn from Jesus' encounter with the Samaritan woman at the well (John 4:1-26)? How can we apply that to our situation with our SSA child?

9. It's hard to admit to ourselves or to others that there may be things we are unwilling to surrender to God. Can you share anything in your life that might fall into that category? (Note: Awareness is half the battle in just about any difficult situation. After awareness comes a choice: to do what is necessary to change that which is within our ability to change, or to keep things as they are. Change is hard, and often it is painful. What are the risks and rewards of both options? The main question is: Is it worth it to change? Or are you okay keeping things as they are? If God is dealing with you in a specific area of surrender, He will see you through it if you will let Him.)

10. God seeks people who will worship Him in Spirit and in truth (John 4:24). Both are equally important. What are the hazards of worshiping only in the Spirit but not truth, or truth but not the Spirit?

11. Your takeaway: If you were to sum up the impact of this week's lesson in one concise thought, what would that be?

12. Do you have any prayer requests pertaining to your child's SSA you would like to share?

Closing Prayer

Father God,

We feel the weight of responsibility in our words, actions, and influence with our children. We want to be Your vessels in their lives, to speak love and life into them, to speak truth saturated in Your love. But we admit that sometimes our agenda, our "flesh" gets in the way, and we mess things up. We don't want to do that anymore, so we choose right now to surrender our children and our relationships with them to You, and to Your will. Holy Spirit, teach us what to say, when and how to say it, and when to keep our mouths shut. Put a guard over our mouths to keep us from saying anything that would unnecessarily hurt our children or damage our relationships with them. Grant us Your wisdom, discernment, and a measure of faith to meet every situation in a manner that honors You. And above all, fill each one of us with Your agape love so that we may love our sons and daughters as You love us. Thank You that You are always with us. Teach us to depend on You more and more.

In Jesus' Mighty Name,

Amen.

Chapter Seven

Self-Care for the Long Haul: Introduction to Healthy Boundaries, Setting Limits, & Support

Jesus replied: "'Love the Lord your God with all your heart and with all your soul and with all your mind.' This is the first and greatest commandment. And the second is like it: 'Love your neighbor as yourself.'"
Matthew 22:37-39

ဢႣ

"We do not lead others into the Light by stepping into the darkness with them."
Melody Beattie, *The Language of Letting Go*[15]

Colorado is a state filled with boundless beauty... and danger. A day trip to the mountains promises peace, beauty, tranquility, and awe. However even a short hike in the amazing Rocky Mountain National Park requires a fair amount of planning and preparation. Too often, vacationers from out of state take off on a trail, enticed by the exhilaration of venturing into some of the most breathtaking views on the planet. Likewise, those same vacationers often end up on the evening news, the subject of yet another harrowing rescue.

The dangers in the mountains are as obvious as potential wildlife threats—yes, we have bears, cougars, and rattlesnakes—but the subtler and less obvious dangers are invisible to the naked eye and catch many people off guard. For example, the altitude alone can be dangerous for some. The air is thin in the higher elevations, the sun is stronger, and dehydration is a very real threat. No one with any amount of knowledge of mountain perils and in their right mind will take off on a hike without first spending some time getting acclimated to the elevation, loading up with water, applying sunscreen and bringing extra. Other good ideas of things to bring: a map, compass, and whistle. Hikers also need to be dressed appropriately. Hiking boots, a hat, rain gear, and sunglasses are essentials. Also, it's always wise to check with the ranger station before hiking to inquire about potential bad weather, snowmelt-swollen rivers, or other life-threatening dangers. Yes, it can snow in the mountains during the summer months here, and summer thunderstorms can bring life-threatening lightning, hail, and flash flooding—suddenly and unexpectedly.

Embarking on this journey of having a child with SSA requires no less preparation and specific attention to your own needs and potential dangers.

What are the dangers for you, as the parent of a child with SSA? Where do we begin?! The most obvious dangers are those associated with the emotional and psychological repercussions of stress, worry, fear, and grief. Stress is a recognized contributor to numerous health issues, including hypertension, heart disease, diabetes, and the list goes on and on. Stress suppresses the immune system and overwhelms the autonomic nervous system and the limbic system (which, in part, affects memory and focus, decision-making capabilities, and regulates hormones, etc.). In short, stress at its very least can make us sick, and at the worst, it can kill. True story: I totaled my car during a particularly stressful time in my life. I hadn't been sleeping well, I was fatigued, and my mind was in a fog; the light turned green, and I simply followed the car in front of me, not realizing the left-turn green *arrow* had turned to a green *yield*. Thankfully no one was seriously injured, but that accident cost me dearly in more ways than one. Worst of all was admitting I was the one at fault. Is it important to manage stress well? You bet! I could have died that day, or worse, I could have killed someone else.

Another serious threat during times of worry, stress, fear, and especially when you feel powerless over a situation (such as your adult child's choice to venture into the world of homosexual sex), is self-medicating your pain. Too many hurting people turn to alcohol or drugs in an effort to ease their emotional pain. Even prescriptions that are helpful when used appropriately may become addictive—or deadly—when misused. For instance, the opioid addiction rate in this country is off the charts. In fact, in 2014 alone, 14,800 drug overdose deaths in the U.S. involved opioid pain relievers.[16] Who are these drug users and addicts? Many of them are housewives, executives, stay-at-home moms, PTA members, and church leaders—people you would never suspect. These people never set out to become drug addicts. What may have started as simply adding a pill now and then to the regular dosage increased slowly over time. Before they realized it, they were hooked. Self-medicating our emotional pain never ends well.

So what is the solution? Two little words…words that may seem over-simple or obsolete: *self-care.* You may be thinking, *but we are Christians; isn't self-care selfish?* In a word: No! Even Jesus practiced self-care. How? He ate when He was hungry. He rested when He was tired. He went to the mountain alone to pray when He needed to refuel spiritually. Known as the Prince of Peace, Jesus lived a peaceful life—in the midst of accusations, traps, and threats from the Pharisees, betrayals from nearly everyone in His life, even His arrest, torture, and eventual death. He knew the secret to living in peace regardless of the chaos going on around Him.

Sure…but He was God, you may say. Yes, that's true, but He was also fully human. His struggle was every bit as real as yours and mine. Even though He was tempted in every way, just as we are, He never sinned (Hebrews 4:15). He knew what it was to face the fiercest temptations, the deepest agony, and the bitter betrayal of nearly everyone He knew. That is why He promised to give us peace—and not just any peace—but *His* peace that surpasses human understanding (Philippians 4:7). In fact, He came to give us that same peace:

*"Peace I leave with you; my peace I give you. I do
not give to you as the world gives.
Do not let your hearts be troubled and do not be
afraid."*

John 14:27

Did you catch that? He *gave* us His peace. His peace isn't anything like what the world gives, but here's the rub: we have to *choose* peace. Thus the admonition to *not let* our hearts be troubled or afraid.

I'm getting ahead of myself. Let's go back to the simple concept of self-care.

What is Self-Care?

The simplest definition of self-care is taking care of *you*. Profound, I know! Have you taken a trip on an airplane in the last 20 years? If so, you may have noticed during the safety instructions before take-off that in the event of a loss of cabin pressure, adults must put their own oxygen mask on first, before assisting a minor child in their care. Why? Because if you try to put it on the child first, and the child is panicked, you could both die. The better plan is for you to put your mask on first. That way, you can breathe and remain calm while you are trying to assist your child. When you put your oxygen mask on first, you save two lives. This is a great picture of self-care.

Self-care is taking care of your *body*. It is eating nutritional food in moderate amounts. It is getting a good night's sleep. It is taking care of your body through physical activity. It is learning to alleviate stress in healthy ways. What's a healthy way to alleviate stress? Take a brisk walk. Vacuum the house. Put on peaceful music—worship music has an especially stress-relieving component. Learn to breathe deep again! Stress often causes us to take shallow breaths, a part of the fight-or-flight response. Taking deep breaths gets oxygen to every part of your body and is beneficial in helping to ease tension.

Self-care is taking care of your *emotions*. No, you don't buy them flowers—or anything else on Amazon.com! But you also don't ignore them, sweep them under the rug, or stuff them down deep. Emotions are a little like toddlers; they will settle for bad attention if good attention is not given to them. For example, grief, hurt, or anger that is stuffed down or ignored may come out in explosive anger or caustic comments. Our emotions always find a way out, just as rays of sunlight shine through the breaks in the clouds. Our deep emotions will seep out or blast out through any crack or crevice or unexpected situation that takes us off guard. Road rage is, in many instances, the result of buried emotions that are not tended to properly. Either we manage our emotions, or our emotions manage us.

What does proper care of your emotions look like? One way may be talking through what you're feeling with a trusted friend, professional life coach, or counselor. It may be pouring out your feelings in your journal, in the quiet of the day when you're alone with your thoughts. There's a saying that "what you don't feel can't heal." We tend to be afraid of our emotions. For example, we may fear that, if we really feel the grief over our child's choice to live the homosexual lifestyle, we will begin to cry and never stop. Or that if we allow ourselves to fully feel the anger and hurt that we will explode into a million pieces or blow up our lives. Neither of these fears is true. When we deal with our emotions at an appropriate time and place, we can safely bring them into the light. Then, and only then, can they be healed.

One of the best ways to care for your emotions is to pour out your heart before God. Open His Word. Find one of those passages in the Psalms where the psalmist is lamenting before God, asking "why?" or simply listing out all the bad things going on in his life. Psalm 34:4-7 is one of my favorites to go to when I'm feeling emotionally overwhelmed:

> *I sought the Lord, and he answered me;*
> *he delivered me from all my fears.*
> *Those who look to him are radiant;*
> *their faces are never covered with shame.*
> *This poor man called, and the Lord heard him;*
> *he saved him out of all his troubles.*
> *The angel of the Lord encamps around those who fear him,*
> *and he delivers them.*

Psalm 91 is another tried and true go-to passage. I find comfort in these words; they remind me to seek God, knowing He hears and responds. He delivers me from my fears. He is my Protector and my Deliverer. The Book of Psalms is full of the emotional plight of the authors, seeking God, and having their needs met as a result. For me—as I am reminded God is for me, He is with me, He sees all, knows all, hears my cries for help, and He is my Rock, my Redeemer, and my Strong Tower—I am able to let all those emotions bubble up to the surface, bring them out of the dark, and into the light of God's tender loving care. I choose to give myself permission to feel them, and then, as a sacrifice of suffering, I choose to give them to Him, knowing He cares for me. He provides the care; but we must choose to let Him.

Boundaries: A Form of Self-Care

Another form of self-care occurs as a result of knowing yourself, what you need, what is not appropriate, safe, or good, and then setting appropriate limits or boundaries. In their book, *Boundaries,*[17] Drs. Cloud and Townsend described boundaries as being *like fences with gates that let good things in and keep bad things out.* Boundaries are not about controlling or manipulating someone else. Boundaries are about you and what you need.

Further, God repeatedly set boundaries in Scripture. He laid out clearly defined guidelines along with a promise of blessings for those who would obey and negative consequences for those who would not. In this way, God gave us the framework for setting boundaries. It is a model we should follow, making appropriate adjustments within the context of our relationships.

Some Basics of Healthy Boundary Setting

As mentioned above, boundaries are not intended to be a method of controlling other people. On the contrary, boundaries provide a clear distinction of what the choices are in a specific scenario, and what the consequences of those choices will bring. Setting a boundary begins when you *recognize what issues* are threatening your peace, safety, etc., or that of your home or family. Once the issue is determined, *the boundary must clearly identify the desired or preferable behavior, or the unwanted/unsafe/unacceptable behavior. Specific consequences* must also be clearly stated in the event the boundary is violated. It *must allow the individual to make a choice* in the situation. There must be a definitive *method of enforcing the boundary,* and finally, *the boundary must be enforced.* You can set boundaries all day long, but if you fail to enforce them, you are letting that person know you don't mean what you say.

For example, if your daughter is upset with you, your boundary may address the issue of being respectful. If the conversation deteriorates into harsh criticism, name-calling, gross exaggerations, passive-aggressive comments, or emotional intensity, take a time out and let her know that you both need time to calm down. Your boundary might be to tell her, *"I can see that you are very angry (hurt, upset, etc.) with me, and I really want to hear what you have to say. However, when I hear harsh criticism, or when you call me names, my emotions escalate, and that's not going to help the situation. Let's take some time to cool off, and when you feel you're able to tell me what's bothering you in a calm, respectful manner, we can work to resolve this situation. I want to resolve this with you. "* If she agrees to your request, the likelihood of coming to a resolution improves greatly. If not, you have a choice to walk away until such time as she can be calm (the consequence). In that way, you're not controlling her; you're simply closing the proverbial gate until she's calm enough that you can let her back into your safe zone.

Setting this type of boundary will not only help to improve your relationships with others in your life, but it will serve to be a training tool for your children that may improve their relationships as well. Also, this type of boundary tells others how you wish to be treated and what is and isn't appropriate within mutually loving, respectful relationships. People will treat us as well or as poorly as we allow them to. They have responsibility for their words and actions, but we also have a responsibility for what we allow into our "gated area." We teach people how we want to be treated through our boundaries or lack thereof.

Depending on the boundary, it is vitally important that, before you set the boundary, you let the other person know how much you care for him. This is especially so whenever the boundary has to do with his SSA. Pad the front end of the conversation with as much love, acceptance, and affirmation of him as you can, and, if necessary, explain to him how his current behavior is impacting you; then restate the positive, affirming, and encouraging points.

Not all boundaries are healthy ones. Unhealthy boundaries include those that are harsh, controlling, manipulative, punitive, or disrespectful to the other person. A healthy boundary between parents and their children will be in the best interests of all parties. We don't have to agree on every aspect of life, however these relationships should be safe, respectful, and loving even in the midst of disagreement. Healthy boundaries are tools to create that kind of safe environment.

To sum it up: the essential elements of boundary setting are: *Expression of sincere love and affirmation* + *identification of the unacceptable/unsafe behavior* + *statement of desired behavior* + *assertion of the potential reward and consequence* + *more love and affirmation*. The final element is *enforcement of the boundary* in the event the boundary is breached.

Boundary setting can feel intimidating in the beginning. If setting boundaries is new to you, start small and test the process a couple of times before broaching a major issue. Healthy boundaries are a vital part of every relationship. As you get better at setting them, you will begin to see an improvement in your relationships and you will be modeling healthy boundary setting for your children. *(If you would like help setting healthy boundaries, please email us at uncommonloveonline@gmail.com. We are here to help.)*

Boundaries of Conscience and Faith & Values

There are other types of boundaries. For example, if your SSA child is living under your care, you may have boundaries that are "if/then" scenarios. One mother told of her adult daughter who was living under her roof. Her boundaries were based on what she would not allow in her home and the consequences of violating those boundaries. One boundary went like this: *There is to be no drinking alcohol in my home. If I discover you are drinking, (then) you will be telling me you no longer wish to live with me, and I will honor your choice to find housing elsewhere.*

A boundary from another mom was similar: *I love you, and you are welcome to continue living in my home. While I care about your (same-sex) girlfriend, I must ask that if the two of you are going to spend time together, that you do so elsewhere. How you spend your time together is your choice, however, I am not okay with you spending time together in my home.* For this mom, allowing her daughter to spend time with her lesbian girlfriend under her roof was enabling sinful behavior, and to do so would be to violate her own faith and values. *No one has the right to expect us to violate our faith and values simply because their faith and values are different.* It's a matter of individuality and respect. We can and should respect our adult children's choices—even if we disagree with them. The other side of that coin is our children should likewise respect our faith and values whether they agree with them or not. It's a matter of mutual respect.

It is important to note, however, that when we put these boundaries out there with our SSA children, we must do so with an overabundance of love, compassion, caring, and kindness. Go the extra mile in affirming your love for your son and your respect for his choices when you present such a boundary. These types of boundaries are not about judging or condemning; they are simply expressions of authenticity that overflow from your individual faith and values. Be prepared for him to be hurt or angry when you set these types of boundaries, but never waver in your affirmations of love, affection, and respect for him.

There is more to this last boundary than simply guarding your faith and values. Let me explain. If you allow your child and his partner to come into your home, for example, you *may be behaving* in a manner that communicates, "I affirm your relationship" *whether that's how you feel or not.* You may be deeply troubled internally when they come to your home together, however, y*our son's assumption may be that you have come around to the notion of him being gay.* His perception may be that you now accept and approve of his homosexuality. Just as our child's perspectives in childhood shaped their reality, the same is true now. With that in mind, it's important to check in with your son periodically to find out what he *perceives* to be your position on his homosexual relationship or lifestyle. If he confirms that it looks as though you have begun to condone his homosexuality, you have inadvertently compromised your faith and values. Take that opportunity to reassert your faith and values in a kind and loving manner, reaffirming your love for him and his partner, and apologize for any confusion you may have caused. Set the record straight, saturating the conversation in love and acceptance of *him*, but without condoning his homosexual behavior.

Whatever boundaries you set, make sure you are clearly communicating your faith and values in the context of unconditional love for your child.

Compromising His values was something Jesus never did. His first priority was to please His Father; everyone else came after. Our priority should be the same. Compromising our faith and values with our SSA kids is like stepping into the dark to lead someone out into the light. It doesn't work unless you take the light with you. As Melody Beattie said in her book, *The Language of Letting Go, "We do not lead others into the Light by stepping into the darkness with them."* We lead them into the Light by letting His Light shine through us. In the beginning, that Light may repel them, because, quite honestly, most of our SSA kids love their darkness, at least on some level (John 3:19-20). What we must realize is *joining them in their darkness (by approving of their sin), while snuffing out the Light in us (suppressing His Spirit and truth), will never help our kids.* We have to be willing to risk their wrath and possible rejection *now*, in the hopes that if we keep letting His Light shine through us, they will hopefully, prayerfully, *someday* return to it. We will explore this topic more in a later chapter. Further, someday we will all have to stand before God at which time we will be held accountable for our actions (Matthew 12:36-37).

Healthy Detachment and Ongoing Support: Other Forms of Self-Care

In Chapter Three we discussed healthy detachment, which is another form of self-care. As a brief review, healthy detachment is a process of determining what you can and can't control, doing what you can regarding the former, and letting go of the latter, then leaving the results in God's hands. It is stepping out of the fray in that moment and taking an emotional step back in order to gain a more objective perspective. It is moving out of the emotional intensity and striving to gain a non-emotional view so as to be able to respond without a knee-jerk response, but instead with a peaceful, grounded response. (For further review, you may want to go back and reread that section in Chapter Three.)

Another type of self-care is finding quality, ongoing support. If you are doing this Bible study with a support group, you are already on track! Make the most of this opportunity to build relationships with those in your group that will last beyond this Bible study. Get to know those in your group who are like-minded and you feel you can trust. Meet outside the group for coffee or dinner. Grow your relationships. (A word of caution: be careful not to choose a married person of the opposite sex to be your support person. Have good boundaries around your emotional and sexual purity.)

Other support may be found through online ministries who specialize in dealing with SSA issues. Some of these ministries provide call-in support groups at no charge. In addition, you may want to find a qualified, caring, and like-minded professional life coach or counselor to talk to on an ongoing basis. There is no shame in reaching out for help. *Everyone* could benefit from quality counseling or professional coaching. Don't let your pride or a sense of shame keep you from seeking sound support. Dealing with the issues associated with having a child with SSA or involved in a homosexual relationship is too big to manage alone. You don't have to do this alone! If you are still unsure where to find help, contact us for referrals.

Before you take that hiking trip to the Rocky Mountains, you need to prepare for the obvious, the inevitable, and the potential. The same is true of embarking on this journey of having a child with SSA. Like previously described in the airplane illustration, if you refuse to heed the instructions of the flight attendant and choose instead to struggle to place the oxygen mask on your six-year-old in the seat next to you, you could both perish. The verses in Matthew 22 at the beginning of this chapter say it best: "Love your neighbor *as yourself*." The assumption here is that we already love (i.e. care for) ourselves. The admonition is that we love our neighbors *in the same way*. If we are not loving and caring for ourselves, and instead are giving everything we have to care for the people around us, at some point we are going to come up empty. When we are empty, who is going to take care of those other people? In order to care for others, we have to take care of ourselves first. It's not selfish. It's common sense, and even Jesus agreed. He modeled and included it as a part of the second greatest commandment. Our responsibility is to go and do likewise.

[NOTE: In the next chapter, we will take a closer look at how to set healthy boundaries.]

DIGGING DEEPER: Journal Questions

1. Do any of the types of self-care cause you to feel uneasy? If so, which ones? Why?

2. Do you feel selfish in taking care of yourself? Do you feel guilt or shame regarding this topic? Why or why not? Take a moment to pray and ask Jesus to reveal His heart to you on this matter.

3. How do you usually manage your emotions? Do you push them down? Try to sweep them under the rug? Do you manage them, or do your emotions manage you? Explain.

4. Do you find yourself blowing up over small or insignificant things? Do you struggle with depression or feeling numb? Each of these could be a sign of not dealing with your emotions in a healthy manner. *(Note: Depression can result from emotional issues or physical ones. If you are feeling depressed, you should not delay in seeing your doctor.)*

5. Do you feel hopeless or despairing of life on a regular basis? Do you have a trusted someone you can talk to? Are you afraid or embarrassed about sharing your feelings? Feelings

are never right or wrong; they simply are what they are. Everyone has times in their lives when their feelings are overwhelming. What's stopping you from reaching out for support?

6. How do you handle stress? Are you a stuffer? An exploder?

7. Take some time to identify your emotions and what events or situations are at the root of what you're feeling.

8. Write out a prayer to God about what you're feeling. Like David, the psalmist, tell God what you're feeling and why. There's no reason to hold back because He already knows. There's nothing you could say that would surprise Him. Telling Him how you're feeling and why is for your benefit. Let it all out. You can trust Him with your feelings. *He cares about you!*

9. Are you willing to set boundaries with your child that may negatively affect your relationship for a time? Why or why not?

10. What boundaries do you need to set with your SSA child? (Note: When you feel that nagging, sick, uncomfortable feeling in your stomach regarding your SSA child, your body— and maybe God—may be trying to tell you something!)

DEEPER STILL: Study Questions

1. Read the following Scriptures. Write down how Jesus was feeling, and how He took care of Himself.

   a. John 4:6

   b. Mark 1:32-35

c.   Luke 5:15-16

d.   Matthew 14:6-13

2.   Read the following Scriptures. Identify what Jesus was
     feeling, and how He responded. (Did He deny His feelings?
     Did He express them? If so, did He do so appropriately or
     inappropriately?)

a.   John 11:17-35

b.   Mark 11:15-16

c.   Matthew 14:14

d.   Mark 3:4-6

e.   Luke 10:20-21

f.   Matthew 26:36-46

3.   God is a God of boundaries. Read the following verses;
     describe the boundary God set forth in each one, and the
     consequence of not respecting that boundary.

a.   John 14:6

b. John 3:5-6

c. John 3:16

d. Galatians 6:7-8

4. Read the following verses and explain the significance of each regarding setting boundaries of conscience:

a. John 3:19-20

b. Matthew 5:14-16

5. It is true that if your child is offended or angered by your boundaries of conscience, she may sever her relationship with you for a time, which would seriously hinder your influence in her life. Are you willing to make that sacrifice in order to not compromise your faith and values? Why or why not?

6. Are you the only person in the world God can use to influence your child? Read Numbers 22:21-34. Who/what did God use to speak to Balaam? What was the result of that conversation? Read Exodus 3:1-4. What did God use in this passage to speak to Moses? What does this say about your influence?

7. If you compromise your faith and values with your SSA child, what might that communicate to your child? What does it say about your faith and values? About who or what your priority is?

8. It is said: "People don't change until it hurts more to stay as they are than it does to change." What might that mean in regard to your SSA child and the decisions you make in your relationship with him?

APPLICATION: Write out your takeaway.

_____

_____

_____

_____

_____

_____

_____

_____

_____

_____

SELF-CARE FOR THE LONG HAUL: INTRODUCTION TO HEALTHY BOUNDARIES, SETTING LIMITS, & SUPPORT

Jesus replied: "'Love the Lord your God with all your heart and with all your soul and with all your mind.' 'This is the first and greatest commandment. And the second is like it: 'Love your neighbor as yourself.'"

Matthew 22:37-39

ℰℛ

"We do not lead others into the Light by stepping into the darkness with them."

Melody Beattie, *The Language of Letting Go*[18]

My family and I used to live within an easy day's drive of Arkansas and the beautiful Ozark Mountains. Every year for several years, we made an annual trip to the charming little town of Eureka Springs. The first year we went as a family we explored every nuance of the town and surrounding area. One of the highlights of the trip was going down into the Onyx Cave. It was "a thousand degrees" outside—at least, it sure felt like it that summer in Eureka Springs, with stifling humidity on top of high heat. But walking down into that cave was refreshing! The temperature in the cave was significantly cooler than it was at street level. The only trouble was, without a lantern you literally couldn't see your hand in front of your face!

I don't know about you, but I haven't been afraid of the dark since I was a kid, but that darkness was terrifying! In a moment, when the lanterns are turned out in a place like that, your mind goes into hyperdrive, imagining every horrible scenario possible. *What if there was a cave-in? There would be no light, no oxygen!* Suddenly, you feel like you can't breathe.

Then your guide instructs you to turn around and look behind you. There in the distance is the faintest hint of light. If the lanterns went out, we would be okay. The way out is there. Simply follow the light.

That's a little bit like the situation our SSA kids are in. They have gone down into the dark world of homosexuality, because for whatever reason, it felt good to do so. (Sin almost always feels good in the beginning, doesn't it?) They may even be telling you it's great there, that they are happy and fulfilled, but, we weren't meant to live out our lives in a cave—even if it is cooler than street level! Secondly, their man-made lanterns (same-sex relationships) could lose their sparkle and shine at any moment. When that happens, they may be terrified. They may feel scared, hurt, alone or trapped, and they won't be able to see their way out. That's when we need to be conduits for the Light of Christ that show them the way.

Hidden or suppressed light cannot affect darkness. Darkness only flees from light that shines into it, but if we hide the Light of Truth, how can it penetrate their darkness? We can shine where we are, even if it appears as just a faint glow from where they are living. Instead, if we condone their homosexual behavior, affirm their choices and compromise our faith, we have snuffed out the Light of truth and hope and have entered the darkness with them. When this happens, and Christ's light in us is hidden or suppressed, what then? What message are they likely to receive, especially if they know we are committed Christians? (They may think, *"If mom's okay with it and she's a committed Christian, then God must be okay with it too."*) In that scenario, how can we be a beacon of light for them to find their way out? Love alone that condones—permissive love—cannot be light that leads out of darkness. Instead, it's like remodeling a man's prison cell with cozy furniture and cheerful curtains on the window. It makes life a bit more comfortable, but he is still in prison.

Ultimately, it is only Christ's light that is going to give our SSA kids hope for a way out. Our part is to stay plugged into the Light Source so that He never ceases to shine through us.

Discussion questions

1. Why is self-care important? What are the dangers of failing to engage in self-care?

2. What challenges, if any, are you facing in regard to self-care? How would you like to engage in better self-care?

3. How is boundary setting a part of self-care?

4. What do boundaries accomplish?

5. Do you have good, solid boundaries with your SSA child? Why or why not?

6. In what areas do you need to set new or better boundaries with your SSA child?

7. Are you willing to compromise your faith and values in order to maintain a relationship with your SSA child? Why or why not?

8. Have you ever violated or compromised your faith and values? How did that feel?

9. Describe what the Melody Beattie quote above means to you.

10. Has God ever used anyone besides your parents to influence your life or faith? If so, who did He use, and how did that change your life?

11. Your takeaway: If you were to sum up the impact of this week's lesson in one concise thought, what would that be?

12. Do you have any prayer requests pertaining to your child's SSA you would like to share?

Closing Prayer

Father God,

*This journey is so hard! We want to do what is right in your eyes **and** what is right for our children. Help us to see those things are one and the same! Help us to trust You with the lives of our children no matter what! Give us Your wisdom and discernment regarding our need to take care of ourselves, to set and enforce boundaries with our children, and to continue fighting this good fight in a way that honors You. Increase our faith in You, our devotion to You, and our determination to please You above all others. Thank You that You can work through even a donkey on behalf of our children if necessary! Thank You that You will never leave or forsake our children or us, and You will never, ever give up on us.*

In Jesus' Mighty Name,

Amen.

Chapter Eight

A Closer Look at Boundary Setting & Embracing the New Normal (Without Giving Up Hope!)

So we fix our eyes not on what is seen, but on what is unseen, since what is seen is temporary, but what is unseen is eternal.

2 Corinthians 4:18

శార్థ

"...let us run with perseverance the race marked out for us, fixing our eyes on Jesus, the pioneer and perfecter of faith. For the joy set before him he endured the cross, scorning its shame, and sat down at the right hand of the throne of God."

Hebrews 12:1b-2

The diagnosis was inoperable brain cancer. It wouldn't take her life immediately; in fact, it might not ever kill her, but she would never be free of it. It would, however, gradually affect her motor skills and other brain activity over the years as the web-like cancer spread to other areas of her brain. It was one of those moments when it felt like getting punched in the stomach.

When we heard the news, we immediately called her to express our love and concern, and to tell her we were praying for her. We were awed by her strength in that moment, and especially when she stated matter-of-factly: "This is simply my new normal."

The New Normal

When a child comes out it's much the same scenario. Although we don't know exactly what the prognosis is—or the length of this journey for our child or our family—it nonetheless changes our lives. Whether we like it or not, we have entered into a new normal. For some, the journey into homosexuality lasts a few years. For others, it can go on for decades. For others still, their child may never be delivered from SSA or the homosexual lifestyle.

The new normal often begins with personality changes and outward appearances. Your once kind, compassionate child may begin to have a sharp edge to her personality. Or the reverse can be true. After having hidden this secret for some time, the relief of coming out may reveal a more relaxed side of her personality. Hairstyles, taste in clothing, and even the way he carries himself may begin to change. Your child may get radical tattoos or unusual body piercings as an expression of what he associates as his true identity. Many times, these changes in outward appearances are their way not only of expressing themselves, but also of coming out to the world without having to actually have that conversation with everyone. Once they have accepted a homosexual identity, they often become proud of it and want to put it out there for the whole world to see.

Another new normal may be the people your child begins to spend time with or date. At some point, your son may move in with his partner, and they may eventually pursue a civil union. Every person is different, so for some, this progression will take years; for others it may happen quickly. Whatever the case, his new normal now ushers you into a new normal as well. Holidays and family get-togethers will be different. Extended family members may make comments—either supportive or condemning. Others will ignore the elephant in the room. Some will openly judge you, or your child, or both, or they may congratulate him on embracing his new identity.

For some of these young adults, they may come out very slowly, cautiously, and privately. For others, once they make the decision to accept this as their identity, they come out in a bold way, posting the news on their Facebook page or tweeting it on Twitter. Once they change their public identity, you, too, are outed, which alters your public identity as well. At this point, you are now known as the parent of a homosexual child. This is your new normal.

Exploring Boundary Issues in the New Normal

As your daughter begins to put herself out there in the dating world, and as she embarks on a relationship with a same-sex partner, you will be faced with a number of different scenarios about which you will have to determine—sometimes without any warning—how to handle. Often the first issue to arise is a holiday gathering. Your son wants to bring his boyfriend to the family's 4th of July picnic. Grandma will be there along with aunts, uncles, and cousins. He wants to know if his boyfriend is welcome. Or maybe it's just your immediate family getting together to celebrate a birthday. Your daughter wants to bring her girlfriend. What will you say?

It pays to consider these types of things before you have to face them. Is your child's partner welcome in your home? If so, what boundaries will you set, if any? Will he or she be accepted as a heterosexual partner would? How do your other children feel about that? This new normal affects them, too.

If your adult son, who lives in another state, wants to bring his boyfriend home for Christmas, is he welcome? Are you okay with them sleeping together in your home? Do you buy the boyfriend gifts in order to include him in the celebration? Will he be invited to be in the family photo?

If your daughter and her partner decide to move in together and invite you over for dinner, how will you respond? Will you accept or decline? If you decline, how will you communicate that? If you accept, what does that communicate to them? If your son decides to enter into a civil union with his partner, do you attend the ceremony? Do you help pay for it if he asks? Do you invite family members?

All of these are potential issues you are going to be faced with as a part of your new normal. Deciding in advance how you feel about each of these issues is important. But how do you know what to do? Where does acceptance of their choice to live this lifestyle cross over into approval of the lifestyle? At what point does compassion for your wounded child cross over into compromising your faith and values?

Only you can decide the answers to those questions, but hopefully you will make that determination based on obedience to God first and foremost.

Does your faith draw a solid line where you love your child without condition but do not condone the behavior? Or does your fear move you to the point of embracing the same-sex partner, celebrating their civil union, and proudly displaying your family photo with your son and his partner holding hands?

How will these decisions affect your relationship with your child? What do these decisions communicate to her about your faith and your perspective of God? No matter where you land on these issues, there will be haters, judgers, and critics. Putting everyone else and their opinions aside, what do you believe, according to God's Word and His character, is the right thing to do? Quite honestly, where you land on these issues may change over time and probably will.

At the end of the day, what does God say on the issue? Should anyone's opinion about these issues be more important than His? Certainly not! God made it very clear that He is to be our Number One priority. We are called to have no other gods before Him, and yes, our children can become idols when we place their opinions and feelings above God's (Exodus 20:3). The greatest commandment is to love God with your whole heart, soul, and mind (Matthew 22:37-40). Further, Jesus made it very clear that neither our parents, spouse, children, siblings, or even our very own lives are to be more important to us than Him (Luke 14:26-27).

But this is my kid's identity, you say. How do I reject my child? Let me be clear: putting God first in your life doesn't mean you are rejecting your child. The questions to ask and seek answers to are the ones we discussed in Chapter 1:

- What does God say about homosexual behavior/sexual immorality?
- What does God say about those caught in sin, and how did Jesus treat them?

- Did Jesus condone the sinful behavior or confront it?

- Did He condemn the person or the sin?

- Did He offer a way out of sin or simply tell them to get over it?

- Did He set definitive boundaries, or did He minimize sin because it's so hard for us fallen humans to fight temptation?

- Did He gloss over our sin because of our obvious weaknesses, or did He express His compassion and understanding yet still hold the line that sin is wrong?

- Did the sinners He hung out with continue in their sin, or did their lives change because of their interactions with Him?

The answers to these questions will help you formulate responses to your "new normal" dilemmas.

The balance we have to strike in dealing with our kids and their homosexual behavior is indeed a delicate one. If we come down too hard on the sin without balancing it with love and compassion, we run the risk of alienating our children unnecessarily. However, if we are too permissive, complacent, or condoning of the behavior without holding the line on the issue of sin, we run the risk of enabling them and becoming accomplices to their sin. Further, if we are too accepting, if our compassion moves into a compromise of our faith and values, two things happen. First, our faith and values lose their impact. If our faith isn't worth fighting for or standing strong in, then how important is it that our children return to it? In that moment, our faith and values no longer mean very much. Second, when we compromise our faith and values, our children are not forced to bump up against the line between right and wrong within the context of their relationship with us. The natural boundary line of discomfort associated with their choices is removed.

Have you ever been a prodigal yourself? Have you ever chosen to sin willfully and then felt the conviction of the Holy Spirit when you were around someone who consistently tries to do the right thing? When you're around people who are committing the same sins you are, you probably don't feel that pang of conviction, or at least not as strongly.

However, if you're the only one in a group of people who would rightly be appalled by your behavior, you feel that tug, and it's uncomfortable.

The conviction a person feels when he is around people with a different set of values and a more committed faith in Christ can be a motivating factor in his heart that draws him out of his sin and back into right relationship with God. Oh sure, the opposite can be true as well. That conviction might just fuel his anger toward you, and he may decide that you are too judgmental, hateful, mean-spirited, etc. Ultimately, he just may sever his relationship with you.

That's the risk we take when we put Jesus first, but here's the thing: if that happens, if your daughter writes you off, and if you have had a solid, close relationship with her in the past, *she is going to miss you.* She is going to miss calling you up or hanging out with you. She is going to hate not being able to pick up the phone and ask for your help with some project she's working on. That grief and longing over a lost relationship with you will bother her; and God can use those feelings of loss to soften her heart and to move her toward repentance.

The opposite can also happen. It is also possible that your son's heart may become harder, and he may begin to make very self-destructive choices, either with or without your approval of his homosexual behavior. By setting boundaries and maintaining your faith and values, you run the risk of him severing his relationship with you and making bad choice after bad choice, leading him into a life of danger, addiction, and other serious consequences. If that happens, are you willing to surrender his life completely to God, even if it means he has to hit bottom? I don't know of many things that would be harder than sitting by while your child self-destructs, but sometimes, because of our stubbornness and because of the intense hold of sin upon us, hitting bottom is just what we need. If he needs to hit bottom in order to return to right relationship with God, are you willing to let that play out? Have you ever had to hit bottom in order to turn your life around, or did someone rescue you before you hit bottom? I've seen both play out, and while it is excruciating to know your child is headed for a face-down-in-the-ditch experience, it's a lot worse for that child to never be allowed to hit bottom and to continue on a bad path as a result. Just as the father of the prodigal son in Luke 15:11-32 let his son go off and live a life of debauchery, we have to let our adult children make their own decisions without stepping in to rescue them— and without changing our faith and values. How might that story have turned out differently if the father had gone after his son and brought him home against his will. Most assuredly his son would have left again, prolonging his time of wild living.

In that parable, the motivation for the son to return home was in coming to the end of his money, his friends, and himself. In short, he was miserable. When he came to his senses, he was able to realize just how low his life had gotten. In that moment, he realized it was better to be a servant in his father's home than to be living on his own, starving while feeding pigs. Put another way, he had hit bottom.

God does the same thing for us. He allows us to make the choice to live in obedience to Him or to our own selfish desires. He lets us hit bottom. He knows for some of us, that's the only way we will ever be able to look up into His face again. That is His example for us, as parents of kids who have chosen to live according to the SSA desires of their flesh. It's not easy to watch them fall and fall hard. Our instinct is to swoop in and save them from themselves if necessary. It takes a lot of strength and self-control to not attempt to rescue them. But the truth is, *we can't rescue them.* Our trying only prolongs their suffering. The question is, are we willing to let them suffer, especially when there is no guarantee they will ever come to their senses? The fact of the matter is that we alone are responsible and accountable for our actions. We cannot change another person, but if we try to rescue them, that's exactly what we are trying to do. *At the end of the day, this isn't about homosexuality at all. It's about their hearts. God wants their hearts—and He wants our hearts too; fully and completely surrendered to Him.* Changing our kids is not our job, it's God's job; and He can do that most effectively when we get out of the way and let Him do what only He can do.

That's where our consistency in and commitment to our faith is paramount. Since the day you found out you were going to be a parent, consistency has been the rule of thumb. When you were pregnant, you needed to be consistent in healthy eating habits, leaving off the junk food and caffeine. When your kids were toddlers, young children, pre-teens, adolescents, and even young adults, consistency was the rule. It was vitally important for you to be consistent in setting and enforcing your boundaries, in your balance of compassion and correction, and in your displays of love and discipline. Why? Because when we are inconsistent, our kids know our boundaries are weak or don't mean anything, and they realize they can run roughshod over us. They learn to manipulate us, to play on our emotions, to make us feel guilty, and to wiggle out of being grounded so that they can go back out and do what got them grounded in the first place! *Bad choices and behaviors* <u>*without consequences*</u> *create a world of hurt for our kids*. If we are consistent in anything, it has to be first that faith and values matter because relationship with God matters; and second, that bad choices bring consequences, and good choices bring rewards. If, as committed Christians, we have openly communicated that our faith and values in Christ matter, and then we approve of their choice to live in willful sin, we are being inconsistent, and our faith and values lose all credibility.

The Issue of Willful Sin

Let's explore the issue of willful sin. All sins are equal at the cross, because every sin requires a blood sacrifice in order for us to be able to enter into relationship with God the Father. Jesus gave Himself as that sacrifice. However, not all sins are the same at their roots or in their subsequent consequences. It is obvious that the consequences of some sins are far greater than those of other sins. However, there is another powerful difference; that difference is revealed by a *choice* to sin versus *unintentionally* sinning. Just like premeditated murder is different than accidental murder in that one is intentional while the other happened without forethought or planning. The end result is the same in that someone lost his life, but the punishment is far more serious for premeditated murder. Why? Because it reveals a darkened heart. Even our humanistic government views these murders differently. The same is true of SSA; having the *desire* for same-sex behavior versus making the *choice* to commit and engage in homosexual sex reveals a completely different heart condition.

Think of it this way. If you have a wreck as a result of talking on the phone while driving, and the driver of the other car dies, you are responsible for that person's death. You did not intend to get in an accident that day, and you certainly didn't intend for anyone to die, but you allowed yourself to get distracted and a life was lost. That is incidental sin. It is still sin, and you are still accountable for it.

However, if you choose to drive with full awareness that you are too drunk to do so safely, and end up killing someone in a car wreck, that is willful sin. Now, you can split hairs over drunk driving versus sexual behavior if you want. Every analogy concerning different sins eventually breaks down, but the point here is the difference between intentional, willful sin and unintentional sin. It is the difference between tripping and falling while walking across a bridge and intentionally jumping off the bridge. One is incidental; the other is intentional and it's called suicide. Both reveal very different heart conditions.

As we discussed previously, homosexual (SSA) desire is a temptation brought about through the convergence of a number of factors in infancy or childhood. It is the perfect storm of a person's wounds lining up with the lies of society and the deceptions of the enemy that result in a distortion of one's sexual desires. It's a little like a child whose parent consistently had fits of rage and violence, subsequently having a panic attack as an adult when her husband yells at her. SSA is a reaction to a set of circumstances that leads the person's sexual identity to become distorted, and this is no fault of the child. Just as the violent abuse that led to the panic attack was not the child's fault. SSA is not a choice. Engaging in homosexual sex, however, *is* a choice. It's one thing to have the desire for homosexual sex and quite a different thing to engage in homosexual sex.

So what is a person with SSA to do? One woman asked me, "So is my child just supposed to be alone and celibate his whole life?" While no parent wants their child to miss out on the wonders of sex or to live alone for the duration of his life, living celibate or alone is not the end of the world. Lots of heterosexual people never marry and never have sex. Lots of divorced people never remarry and never have sex again.

Is that so awful? Which is worse? To live a pure life that is pleasing to God without sex, or to have sex outside of God's design and live a life that is not pleasing to Him? I can say this with certainty: people who never have sex don't get sexually transmitted diseases. They don't get pregnant outside of marriage, and they don't suffer through the horror and lifelong pain of abortion. They are at almost no risk of getting AIDS or HIV. They are at no risk of getting HPV (Human Papilloma Virus), which sometimes causes cancer, and the list goes on.

What are the risks of *not* having sex? Sadness, loneliness, and depression come to mind, but intentionally living a life of purity in order to please God comes with benefits that can far outweigh those feelings. In fact, if we are living our life for God, we may be serving Him in ways that keep us from feeling sad and getting depressed. Do we know what the statistics for suicide for single virgins are? No. Why? Because to my knowledge, there has never been a need for such a study. What is the suicide rate for homosexual men? It is about six times higher than heterosexuals.[19]

The point is this: are we really going to say that it is better to sin against God and our own bodies than to live a life of celibacy (1 Corinthians 6:18)? Can you say *compromise*?

Here's another bit of truth to consider. A number of homosexuals who have willingly chosen to abandon their lifestyle out of obedience to God have actually gotten married to a heterosexual person. As a result, they have lived happy and fulfilled lives, have remained married, and have had children. The principle here is that *God honors our obedience*. Sometimes He takes the SSA away completely. Sometimes, the person makes a choice to be obedient, and God works out the details without removing the desire for homosexual sex. Can a homosexual live a happy and fulfilled life in a heterosexual marriage? Absolutely! If God can create this vast, unsearchable universe by speaking it into existence, don't you think He can give someone with SSA a happy, fulfilled life in a heterosexual marriage? How small is our faith if we concede that the best option for a satisfying life is to willfully sin against God?

No, it wouldn't be easy to make the choice to live a life of celibacy or to live in a heterosexual relationship when you have SSA, but what scenario in life is without pain and difficulty? Many of us have believed the lie that those with SSA are repulsed by the opposite sex. However even the LGBT community has refuted this notion, confirming that sexuality/sexual desire is "fluid" (which means it can change over time). What it all boils down to, then, is, "where is God in our priorities?" Is He Number One, or is my sexual desire number one? One of those priorities promises that *even in hardship, God blesses.* The other priority promises pain upon pain and consequence upon consequence in addition to grieving the Holy Spirit.

The bottom line is what God does in the life of a person whose heart is fully His. Story after story in Scripture proves that nothing is impossible with God. Therefore, the question remains: *Who do you say He is?* Is He permissive? Is He harsh and uncaring, or is He good, even when things go terribly wrong? Once again, we prove what we believe by the way we choose to live when life gets hard. Will you compromise what you know is right (according to God's Word) in order to maintain a close relationship with your SSA child? If so, what does that say about your faith and the size of your God?

God doesn't want or need us to compromise His principles or our faith in order to reach our prodigal kids. On the contrary, He wants us to give our hearts to him fully, by faith—faith that comes from His Spirit and that lines up with His Word; the faith our children have known us to live by and to revere; the same faith about which we have taught them.

As you're trying to decide how to handle all those issues that will be or have been coming your way regarding your "new normal," consider giving your heart fully to God in faithfulness and obedience. Put Him first, and He will work out the rest. It may be hard. It will probably be painful. You may even lose your relationship with your child for a time, but the Christian life isn't about getting our ticket to heaven when we die and living however we want until then.

Living the Christian life requires faith, commitment, and sacrifice; and most of all, it requires putting God first, surrendering what we want or what we think is best, and living according to the principles He laid out for us in His Word and by His Spirit within us. It requires we do this out of sincere love for Him—not by trying to earn His approval or by adhering to the letter of the Law. (Remember: what He speaks to our spirit will always line up with His written Word. If ever the two are in conflict, always follow His written Word.)

The question is: *what will you choose?* Choose carefully, for how you choose to live *will* influence your child. Will you choose to put God first and exemplify what it means to live a life of faith, or will you put your child first? God will never force His way upon you. The choice is yours.

Holding Onto Hope...In Our New Normal

So how do we hold onto hope when our lives have changed so dramatically? How do we hold onto hope when our SSA child believes this is who he is now; that his entire identity is defined by his same-sex attraction? How do we hold onto hope when the world around us confidently states, "they are born this way?" First, let's discuss what that hope is.

Because homosexual behavior/sexual immorality is a sin, and because it is a choice, we can conclude it is not God's will. There is nothing about homosexuality that pleases God because it is sin. Period. With that said, what sin is beyond God's ability to remedy? What life is beyond His ability to redeem, restore, or rebuild? The answer to these questions is none. There is no situation *or* circumstance *or* sin on this planet from which it is impossible for God to deliver His people. Therein lies our hope.

Our greatest hope is that God will deliver our child from SSA—from the desire for homosexual relationship. Our "at the very least" hope is He will move upon our child's heart in such a way that she will abandon her choice to sin whether the SSA desire ever goes away or not. These hopes are vital. Why? When we give up on these hopes, we give up standing in the gap for our kids. As we discussed in a previous chapter, they need us to stand in the gap for them for as long as they are trapped in their sin.

Hope requires faith, and it often requires support. This is why we need each other in this battle. We need one another to encourage us and prop us up when our hope begins to slip away. Regardless of how your child's or your life has changed, God is able to redeem, restore, and return to you and your family what the enemy has endeavored to steal. If you give up hope on your son, the enemy wins. Don't let the enemy win in your family or in his life. Do what you can; hold onto hope for his restoration and deliverance from homosexuality. Continue to stand in the gap for him, and when you feel hope slipping away, reach out to someone who understands.

God loves our children even more than we do, and a life of homosexual sin is not His design for them. How do I know this? Because Jesus came that we might be set free from sin, and indeed, when He gave His life on the cross in payment of our sins, He did just that. When we (and our children) trusted Christ for our salvation, the power of sin over us *was broken*. Even if your daughter has walked away from God, He has not walked away from her. His desire for her is wholeness, righteousness, and an abundant life with Him. Stand in the gap for her; pray for God to soften her heart, to release her from the lies of our culture, from the wounds in her heart, and from the deceptions of the enemy. Pray and never stop praying. God sees. He hears. He knows. He understands, and His heart is for her restoration. Partner with Him, and never ever give up hope. This is the race that has been assigned to us. Let's run it with perseverance, without giving up (Hebrews 12:1b.-2)!

DIGGING DEEPER: Journal Questions

1. How is your 'new normal' different from your old normal?

2. If your public identity has changed since your child came out, how do you feel about that? How have you handled it? Have you expressed your feelings about how your child's coming out has affected you? Why or why not?

3. Pray and ask God to show you areas where you may be placing your child as a priority above Him, and/or where you may be compromising your faith by condoning your child's behavior. Write out any areas He brings to mind.

4. Where is the line, for you, between acceptance of your child's choices and his journey, without approving of the sin, or put another way, having compassion for him without compromising your faith? Is that line in keeping with Christ's example? Why or why not?

5. If you change the phrase from *acceptance without approval* to *compassion without compromise*, does that change where you draw your line with your SSA child? Why or why not? If so, how does it change where you draw your line?

6. One of the hardest things to do as a parent is to see your child suffer. Even harder is to watch them suffering because of their own wrong decisions, and to not step in to make the suffering stop. Have you ever had to 'hit bottom' because of your own wrong choices before turning your life around? How would that situation have likely turned out if someone had rescued you before you hit bottom?

7. What are some situational boundaries you need to set with your SSA child?

DEEPER STILL: Study Questions

1. Read Mark 10:17-31. Anything more important than God in our lives is an idol. What was more important to the wealthy man than eternal life spent with God? Did Jesus run after him and try to persuade him? What did Jesus do? Jesus never shied away from sinners, but He never glossed over their sin either. He draws the boundaries, and then He lets us choose how we will live. He never rescued, enabled, or compromised on any issue, much less that of sin.

2. Read Isaiah 5:20. Our culture insists that homosexuality is good and that those who refuse to embrace it are evil. What does God say about sexual immorality, and particularly

about homosexuality? Read Romans 12:9. What does this say about good and evil?

3. Given that sin hurts the sinner (and others), and given that God's love is designed to move people towards seeking Him and to foster love for Him, is homosexual behavior in any way good, acceptable, or pleasing to God (See Romans 1:21-27)?

4. Read 1 Corinthians 7:7-8. What is the message about marriage and celibacy Paul is relating here? How could this apply to our SSA kids?

5. Read Ezekiel 36:26-29a. Can one who loves his sin, be moved toward reverent love for a perfect and sinless (righteous) God through that sin? How? What does this say about where we place our hope?

6. Read Hebrews 12:1b.-2. As we hold onto hope and stand in the gap for our kids, we will be tempted to measure what God is doing or not doing based on the circumstances in our children's lives. But who must we continually look to in order to maintain our focus and our hope? What was the joy set before Christ in these verses?

7. The story of the prodigal son is found in Luke 15:11-32. Where was the son when he "came to his senses?" What did it take for him to come to his senses? Are you willing to

allow your child to endure something equally as difficult in order to come to his senses? If not, why not?

8. Read Matthew 9:9-13. Christ is our example for loving sinners without condoning sin. How do you apply His example to this situation with your SSA child? What, according to this passage, did Jesus come to do?

9. Read John 12:46-48. In your own words, tell what Jesus said in this passage that He came to do and not to do.

10. We tend to think about God's wrath in relationship to the Old Testament. What does Romans 2:4-6 say about God's wrath? Why does He hate sin? How should this motivate us to pray for our children caught up in sin?

11. Read Galatians 5:1. From what did Jesus come to set us free? What is the verb tense in the first sentence of this verse (Past? Present? Future?)? Why is that verb tense important?

12. Also in relation to Galatians 5:1, what is the directive given in response to the freedom Jesus has given us? (We can't make this choice for our children, but we can stand in the gap for them, pray God will change their heart's desire, and as a result, that they will make the right choice.)

13. Who does our child's deliverance depend upon? Read Mark 10:18. What does this verse say about "good" people? Who alone can change the human heart? How does free will play into their deliverance from sin?

APPLICATION: Write out your takeaway.

_____

_____

_____

_____

_____

_____

_____

_____

_____

_____

_____

_____

_____

_____

_____

_____

A Closer Look at Boundary Setting & Embracing the New Normal (Without Giving Up Hope!)

So we fix our eyes not on what is seen, but on what is
unseen, since what is seen is temporary, but what is
unseen is eternal.

2 Corinthians 4:18

࿇

"...let us run with perseverance the race marked out
for us, fixing our eyes on Jesus, the pioneer and per-
fecter of faith. For the joy set before him he endured
the cross, scorning its shame, and sat down at the
right hand of the throne of God."

Hebrews 12:1b-2

The storm came up quickly and violently. The boat was thrashing about, threatening to throw anyone overboard who wasn't holding on tight or strapped down securely. The disciples were terrified! Jesus had stayed behind on the shore to pray, so they were on their own.

Then out of the blackness of the night, and by the flashes of lightning, they saw a figure coming toward them on the water. Thinking it was a ghost, they cried out in fear.

But the figure wasn't a ghost; it was Jesus, and He was coming to save them. He told them to take courage and not be afraid; it was their Rabbi. He had the situation in hand.

As always, Peter, the impulsive one, shouted back at Jesus, "If it's really You, tell me to come to You on the water." To which Jesus replied, "All right; come on."

Peter eased out of the thrashing boat, testing the water with one toe, then five, then the ball of his foot until he knew he could stand on the water. Stand. On the water. What?

As Peter began putting one foot in front of the other, his gaze was transfixed on Jesus, and his fear melted away. Their eyes locked until an especially huge wave came crashing into Peter. Suddenly his focus shifted from the One who gave him the ability to walk on the water, back to the storm with its booming thunder, violent waves, and gale-force wind, and Peter became afraid again.

That's when it happened. Peter, nicknamed The Rock, started sinking...like a rock.

"Lord, save me!" Peter cried out, panic altering the pitch of his voice.

Immediately, Jesus reached down and lifted Peter from the water. As they stepped into the boat, suddenly the storm died down; peace and calm returned to the sea (Luke 14:22-33).

Was the storm still raging when Peter stepped out of that boat? Yes. As long as he maintained his focus on Jesus, Peter was able to walk on the water as though it were a beach. But the very instant he took his eyes off Jesus, Peter sank like a rock.

The same is true of you and me on this journey with our SSA kids. As long as we keep our eyes on Him, we can walk through this storm without fear. It's when we lose focus on Jesus and start looking at the storm that we, too, will sink like a rock.

Discussion Questions

1. Have you ever thought about the fact that by coming out, your child also outed you? If your child has come out, how has that changed your life? If he hasn't, how do you think his doing so

will change your life? How has your normal changed? What emotions does this new normal stir up in you?

2. How have you adjusted to your new normal? What parts are still hard? What can make all the difference as you go forward?

3. This week, did you identify any areas in which you may be placing your child and/or your relationship with your child above God? Are you willing to give your heart fully to God, making Him the priority over your child? Why or why not? If so, what will that look like and how might that improve the situation? Read and discuss Luke 14:26-27.

4. Where is your line between having compassion for your wounded child and compromising your faith? Did this lesson make you rethink where your line is? If so, explain.

5. *Enabling* and *accomplice* are two very strong words. How did those words impact you this week?

6. From this point forward, are you willing to allow your child to 'hit bottom' in the hopes she will come to her senses, even if it means losing your relationship with her for a time, or will you take steps to rescue her? Where is your hope (who are you focusing on?) in these hard circumstances?

7. What boundaries do you have with your SSA child? What boundaries do you feel you need to set?

8. According to God's Word, is there anything good about homosexuality? Have you allowed the world's view of homosexuality to seep into your perspective of it? If so, how?

9. Galatians 5:1 says that Jesus *has set* us free from sin (past tense). How then do our children get free from this stronghold of homosexual sin? Is it up to them? Who changes the desires of our hearts? Where does free will fit into this scenario?

10. Your takeaway: If you were to sum up the impact of this week's lesson in one concise thought, what would that be?

11. Do you have any prayer requests pertaining to your child's SSA you would like to share?

Closing Prayer

Father God,

We admit that we hate how our children's homosexuality has redefined our normal! There are days when we are really angry, and others when we are sad and feel defeated. Father, You know our hearts and our children's hearts even better than we do, and according to Your Word, You hate this sin that has altered all our lives. Direct our hearts, soften the hard places, heal the wounded places, and restore to us what the enemy has stolen, Father. Give us wisdom as we set boundaries with our children, and anytime we are tempted to rescue them, convict us by Your Spirit within us. Father, we don't want to do anything that would prolong the way out of homosexuality for our children. Give us the courage to surrender them to You when everything in us is crying out to rescue them. We entrust our children to Your care, Father, knowing You love them more than we do, You hate their sin more than we do, and You alone are able to deliver them from this sin. Strengthen us for this journey and intervene in their lives for their good and for Your plans and purposes. Help us to run this race, to stay the course, and to keep our focus on You, not on the circumstances. Help us not to lose hope, Father, or to compromise our faith in You. Heal our wounds and our families, Father, for Your glory and honor, and for Your Name's sake.

In the Mighty Name of Jesus,

Amen.

Chapter Nine

HOLDING ONTO HOPE

May the God of hope fill you with all joy and peace
as you trust in Him, so that you may overflow with
hope by the power of the Holy Spirit."
Romans 15:13

℘℃

"As long as there is life, there is hope."
Paraphrase of Ecclesiastes 9:4a.

℘℃

For no word from God will ever fail."
Luke 1:37

Our God has many names. One of my favorites is "the God of hope." Ours is not a God who ends any story with dust and ashes. He doesn't leave things broken or unfinished. He doesn't leave the game when His team is on the bottom. He never concedes. He never quits. He never fails. In fact, because He has given us a glimpse into the final chapters of life on earth, we know that in the end, He defeats the enemy, completely, irrevocably, and for all of eternity. Hope is what He sent His Son to give us—along with continual access to the

Father, freedom from sin, grace when we fail, mercy when we deserve condemnation, salvation that can't be undone, and hope that never disappoints (Romans 5:2; Isaiah 49:23b.). The mere fact that we, as believers, have the Holy Spirit within us means we possess Living Hope within us.

Here are just a few things we possess because of the God of hope:

- Strength and courage – Psalm 31:24
- Help in times of need and protection in the battles of life – Psalm 33:20
- His unfailing love that is always with us – Psalm 33:22
- An eternal inheritance and justice – Psalm 37:34; Isaiah 51:5
- Rest from the weariness of this life – Psalm 62:5
- Confidence and peace in any situation – Psalm 71:5; Romans 5:1
- Renewed strength to keep going no matter what – Isaiah 40:31
- Deliverance from eternal death and separation from God – 2 Corinthians 1:10
- Eternal life as His heirs – Titus 3:7
- An anchor for our soul – Hebrews 6:19
- Healing for our wounds – Isaiah 53:5; 1 Peter 2:24
- Hope for healing for the brokenhearted, freedom for captives, release for prisoners, comfort for those who mourn; everlasting joy in exchange for mourning, shame, and disgrace; praise instead of despair, and restoration and renewal of that which has been broken down, destroyed, and left in ruins (Isaiah 61: 1-7; Luke 4:18-19)

A lot of people in this world will tell you that because your son has Same-Sex Attraction, there is no hope that he will ever be heterosexual. A lot of people believe our kids were born this way, and they may even suggest that God made them this way because they believe He has no problem with homosexuality. But what does God say? What did Jesus *do*? In His short three years of ministry on this earth, how many illnesses did He heal? How many people were brought back to life after experiencing death? We have looked extensively into these questions in previous chapters. Jesus walked on water. He proved that even the wind and the waves and the fish of the sea do His bidding. God spoke through a donkey and sent angels to minister and speak to His servants. Twice He protected a single child from evil men who ordered the killing of countless children in order to thwart God's plans. He caused the sun to stand still. He parted the Red Sea and the Jordan River—while at flood stage. He brought 10 plagues to Egypt to prove His power and to set His people free from Pharaoh. He provided water from a rock, manna from heaven, and quail to feed His chosen people as they wandered in the desert. He still causes the sun to rise and set each day, the moon to orbit the earth, and the seasons to come and go on His timetable. In fact, He *spoke* this vast, unsearchable universe into being. What then is impossible for Him? He answered that question directly for us, in three separate instances and in three different ways: *Matthew 19:26, Mark 10:27, and Luke 18:27—all of which basically communicate the same truth:*

"What is impossible with man is possible with God."
Luke 18:27

In two of these three verses the word *all* is used. What does *all* mean here? It means ALL.

Is the sexual attraction of your child bigger than any of these things? In a word: no. Nothing in all of creation is beyond God's ability to heal, redeem, restore, or rebuild. Nothing.

So you may be thinking, "Well ... so God *can*, but *will* He?" I can't promise that He will. Likewise, you can't know He won't! This is where hope comes in. If we believe God can heal our children's wounds and restore natural attraction to them, and we intercede for our children, asking God to do that, we can continue hoping that He will. He may deliver some of our children overnight, completely. Or He may choose to heal and deliver them after we are gone from this earth. He may bring them out of the homosexual lifestyle without delivering them from SSA, and some of them may never come out of homosexuality. But hope does not require that we know. Hope only requires we believe the God of the Universe who hates sin and who loves our children even more than we do CAN heal and deliver them. As long as there is life, there is hope. And as long as there is hope, we continue standing in the gap. That is why hope is so important! It keeps us fighting for our kids.

The Cost of Hope

There is a cost for continuing to hold onto hope, and it can be a high price indeed. In the event it takes decades for your child to be set free from homosexuality, you will have to continually battle discouragement, despair, frustration, grief, and hopelessness. These things will dog you, and if you aren't pressing into God daily, and reaching out to others who understand and will help to prop up your hope, you're going to struggle with these feelings. Hope is incredibly fragile. If you aren't diligent, these feelings can crush your hope and destroy your resolve. For most of us, this will be a long journey, and that is why we need each other.

Another cost of holding onto hope is the impact doing so will have on your relationships with your SSA child, his partner, other family members and friends who disagree with your position. Add to that our society that is swift to accuse, shame, blame, and bully those who do not condone homosexuality. You will regularly be bombarded with attacks from the enemy and from our culture. Further, if your son realizes you are hoping for him to someday leave the homosexual lifestyle, he will most likely be deeply hurt. Once again, your relationship with your son may also be at risk when he is faced with the reality that not only do you not condone his sexual behavior, but on some level, you are hoping for his relationship with his partner to end. Rest assured, this may very well be a devastating blow to him.

In that moment, you will probably be tempted to roll back your disapproval of the sin and your hope for his return to natural sexual desire in order to restore the relationship. I truly understand the pull to want to do that, but doing so carries its own potential costs—costs we have discussed at length previously. All you can do in these circumstances is to love your son the best way you know how. Reassure him you don't want him to be hurt and refuse to get into the details of why you hope for his freedom from SSA. Remember, if you entrust the situation to God, surrendering every aspect of it to Him, He will honor your faithfulness. He will carry you through the hard days and nights. He will grow your faith, and you will experience blessings in unexpected ways.

One thought we must keep in mind in these times of overwhelming loss and pain is that the world around us—what is seen—is temporary; it is only a façade. What really matters are the hearts and lives—the unseen and invisible spiritual lives—of the people in this world in relation to their position with God. Do they know Jesus? Are they walking in obedience to God, or are they living in rebellion? Are they wounded by this world and deceived by the enemy who seeks to kill, steal, and destroy them? If so, Jesus is their only hope! And if we are truly His, by fighting the enemy on their behalf, by living our lives in a way that points them to God's love, grace, forgiveness, hope, and restoration—even if it costs us our relationship with our children *for a time*—we are fighting *for* them. That is an uncommon love. Scripture puts it this way:

> *"Therefore, since through God's mercy we have this minis-*
> *try, we do not lose heart. Rather, we have renounced secret*
> *and shameful ways; we do not use deception, nor do we*
> *distort the word of God. On the contrary, by setting forth*
> *the truth plainly we commend ourselves to everyone's con-*
> *science in the sight of God... All this is for your benefit, so*
> *that the grace that is reaching more and more people may*
> *cause thanksgiving to overflow to the glory of God. There-*
> *fore we do not lose heart. Though outwardly we are wast-*
> *ing away, yet inwardly we are being renewed day by day.*
> *For our light and momentary troubles are achieving for us*
> *an eternal glory that far outweighs them all. So we fix our*
> *eyes not on what is seen, but on what is unseen, since what*
> *is seen is temporary, but what is unseen is eternal."*
>
> 2 Corinthians 4:1-2, 15-18

The question each one of us must wrestle with is: Will I believe God and continue to place my hope and trust in Him? Will I put God first in my life in order to fight for my child? Or will I put my child first and rebel against the only One who can set him free? As I said in an earlier chapter, how we respond to our circumstances reveals where we are in our walk with God. As uncomfortable as this set of circumstances is, God has allowed it to trespass in your life for a multitude of purposes—one of which is to refine you; it is not to harm you or your child, but to make you more like Jesus. In every difficult circumstance in our lives, one of the primary things God wants to do is to reveal Himself to us in a new way—a way that strengthens our faith and trust in Him, and our impact in this world.

The Call to Perseverance

The fight we are embroiled in is not for the faint of heart. It will be a painful journey, replete with pitfalls, battles, losses, setbacks, discouragement, fears, crises, and challenges of all kinds. But it is a good fight! It is a fight of faith on behalf of everyone around us. What we do, what we say, how we behave, the choices we make—everything in our lives is a choice for faith in God or against Him.

> *"But you, man of God, flee from all this, and pursue righteousness, godliness, faith, love, endurance and gentleness. [12] Fight the good fight of the faith. Take hold of the eternal life to which you were called when you made your good confession in the presence of many witnesses. [13] In the sight of God, who gives life to everything, and of Christ Jesus, who while testifying before Pontius Pilate made the good confession, I charge you [14] to keep this command without spot or blame until the appearing of our Lord Jesus Christ."*
>
> 1 Timothy 6:11-14

The good news is we never have to fight this fight alone! Our God goes before us and with us (Deuteronomy 31:6). Indeed, the battle is His (1 Samuel 17:47). If we will stand firm in faith in and obedience to Him, He will fight for us (Exodus 14:13-14).

One of God's promises to us is that He will finish the work He has begun in us and in our children (Philippians 1:6). Our part is to hold onto the hope we have in Jesus Christ, with faith, obedience, and perseverance, entrusting the outcomes to Him. It's not easy. It never will be. But God is good and kind and trustworthy; He is patient and loving, and He knows what we need before we even ask. If we can remember all this is His story—that both our children and we are characters in His story—and He has already written the ending—then perhaps we can finish this race well.

A Word About Free Will

Anytime there is an issue of praying for another person to be set free or delivered from a particular sin, the question of free will arises. One of the overriding principles of the Christian faith is that of man's free will. Another is the principle of God's sovereignty. Both are true aspects of our faith, but what happens when man's free will bumps up against God's sovereignty? Let's say for example, that Kelly, a single woman, gets pregnant, and her boyfriend and the baby's father, Kyle, wants her to have an abortion. Now let's also suppose God has a specific purpose for that baby to fulfill as an adult. Kelly reluctantly gives in to Kyle's pressure and goes through with the abortion. The abortion fails, however, and the child is born alive. Or maybe they arrive at the clinic and it's closed for business because the entire staff came down with the flu. Given more time to consider the decision, Kelly decides to save the life of her child. It was Kyle's free will to coerce Kelly to abort their baby, and Kelly's free will to give in to Kyle's coercion, but God's sovereign will superseded both. The outcome reflected God's sovereignty instead of Kyle or Kelly's free will. The point here is that, yes, we do have free will. We have the ability to choose to do this or that, to obey God or not, to rob a bank or buy an ice cream cone. However, when our choice would prevent God's sovereign will from occurring, God intervenes as only He can, and His will prevails. If that weren't the case, God wouldn't truly be sovereign, would He? Sovereignty literally means *the top authority*. Kings are sovereign. They make decrees, and the entire kingdom either obeys or suffers the consequences. God is sovereign over all (Daniel 5:21). All means ALL! That means God's sovereign will eclipses our free will when necessary.

A biblical example of this is the conversion of Saul of Tarsus, later known as Paul. Saul was a highly educated Jewish man who was quickly rising in the ranks of the Pharisees. We first see him holding the coats of the men who stoned Stephen to death in Acts 7:54-60. In the very next chapter, Saul begins to persecute Christians himself, having both men and women arrested, flogged, imprisoned, and having some killed. At the beginning of Acts chapter 9, Saul is passionately continuing to threaten Jesus' disciples, when he embarks on yet another mission of persecution to the city of Damascus. But as he neared the city of Damascus, as you probably know, Saul encountered the resurrected Christ. Jesus didn't say much to Saul; He didn't need to! As a result of this encounter, Saul (soon after called Paul), became one of the most fervent and passionate apostles, eventually heading up the very group of Christians he sought to destroy, and who later penned several letters which became key books of the New Testament. Did Saul set out that day to become a Christian preacher? No way! But God chose him for that role, and let's just say God gets His way when it is important for Him to do so.

In the case of our children with SSA, they certainly have free will about the choices they make. However, our sovereign God specializes in transforming hearts and minds and setting captives free. Of course, there is no guarantee God will set your child free from SSA or the homosexual lifestyle, however we do know (1) God hears the prayers of His people, (2) God hates sin, and (3) because of His agape love He desires the very best for His children. Therefore, we have no reason *not* to pray for our children's deliverance and every reason *to hope and pray* for it!

Ultimately, *"it is God who works in you to will and to act in order to fulfill his good purpose* (Philippians 2:13). We keep asking God to heal their wounds, to deliver them from the deceptions of the enemy, and to restore natural sexual desire to them. We keep seeking His will for our children, and with perseverance, we keep knocking at His proverbial door until He answers (Matthew 7:7-8).

DIGGING DEEPER: Journal Questions

1. Are you hopeful your child will be delivered from SSA or come out of homosexuality? Why or why not?

2. If you are hopeful, what can you do to maintain hope, even if this season in your child's life goes on for decades?

3. If your child never comes out of this lifestyle, what does that say about God? Does that mean He betrayed you or let you down?

4. Do you have the faith you need for this journey? Explain.

5. Take a few minutes to sit quietly before the Lord, and ask Him what He wants you to learn, or how He wants you to change through this process. Write out what you sense God is saying to you.

6. It's natural when bad things happen in our lives for us to feel angry, cheated, betrayed, etc. Do you feel God has let you down in the past? Do you need to do business with Him on that issue?

7. Do you trust God? Why or why not?

8. In what ways has God been faithful to you in your life? List these things in your journal.

9. Have you ever seen God do the impossible in your life or the life of someone close to you? How does that affect your faith in this situation? Often we can have a lot of faith for other people, but when it comes to our situation, we falter and become fearful. Ask God to strengthen your faith, then cooperate with Him. Rehearse the ways He has been faithful to you and refuse to give in to fear and doubt. Write out your thoughts on this in the form of a prayer.

DEEPER STILL: Study Questions

1. Read Romans 15:13. List the good things in this verse that God wants to fulfill in you. Then list all you need to do to receive those things according to this verse. What does "the God of hope" mean?

2. Read Isaiah 61:1-7. This passage is a prophetic description of what Messiah Jesus came to do. Make a list of the things He came to accomplish. To your knowledge, did He accomplish each one? Does this strengthen your faith, or do you dismiss any hope that His past accomplishments in Scripture mean anything to your life and situation? Explain.

3. Read Isaiah 49:23b. What does this verse say about hoping in God? Do you believe this? Why or why not?

4. Answer the following questions in regard to 2 Corinthians 4:1-18.

   a. What, in this passage, helps us to not lose heart?

   b. How many times does the passage mention losing heart?

   c. What does this passage say that we should renounce and what tactics should we refuse to use? (verse 2). Instead, what should we use?

d. Who is the 'god of this age?' Is he more powerful than God the Father? (v. 4)

e. Whose light shines through us? What does that light accomplish? (v. 5-6)

f. Sum up verses 7-12 in your own words.

g. Regarding the inward and the outward, which is always more important? (v. 16)? Why?

h. Read Isaiah 40. How does your "light and momentary trouble" compare to what God has done in the past and what He can still do today? Do you believe God? How can you reframe it in a manner that enables you to continue to persevere?

i. What are we instructed to "fix our eyes on" in verse 18? Why? How do we do that for the long haul?

5. What is God's promise to us in Philippians 1:6? Does that give you hope?

6. Write out Philippians 2:13. What does this verse mean?

7. Read Psalm 33:15. What significance does this verse have in regard to your SSA child? In regard to you?

APPLICATION: Write out your takeaway.

_____

_____

_____

_____

_____

_____

_____

_____

_____

_____

_____

_____

_____

_____

_____

_____

_____

HOLDING ONTO HOPE

*"May the God of hope fill you with all joy and peace
as you trust in him, so that you may overflow with
hope by the power of the Holy Spirit."*
Romans 15:13

ഇൻ

"As long as there is life, there is hope."
Paraphrase of Ecclesiastes 9:4a.

ഇൻ

"For no word from God will ever fail."
Luke 1:37

One of the most hope-destroying aspects of this journey comes from the doubters you will encounter. People are most often negative and discouraging when it comes to the idea of hoping your child will be delivered from SSA or choose to come out of the homosexual lifestyle. Often their negativity is a result of either their own situation with an SSA person, or out of their motivation to get you to accept the situation as it is—either for personal reasons, a need for commonality with you, or simply because they don't believe it is possible. However, the reality is there are *many* stories of people who have either been delivered completely from SSA or who have simply chosen to honor God with their bodies, either remaining celibate or entering into a heterosexual marriage. My encouragement to you is to look for those stories, especially when you are feeling discouraged. They are out there, and they're not hard to find.

Why would someone want to rain on your hope? The sad fact is some people find comfort in knowing that other people's children have also not come out of homosexuality. In some strange way, it makes them feel better about their own situation. It's human nature. The adage that *misery loves company* is true. They don't promote their belief in order to harm you, and many times they don't even do so consciously. Keep this in mind when detractors come along.

Another thing to remember is that no matter how happy or well-adjusted your child may seem, the homosexual lifestyle is a painful one, and quite honestly, it cannot satisfy. How do I know that? To begin with, it is sin. While that sin may feel good in the moment, as a lifestyle, it cannot help but bring pain. Second, not even heterosexual relationships can completely satisfy! Further, if anything on this planet was truly able to satisfy, we wouldn't need Jesus! Add to this the fact that homosexuality is a distortion of God's natural design for sexuality, and there is no way a lifestyle founded on unnatural sex can satisfy (Romans 1:26-27). Never forget these facts!

Thankfully, our hope does not rest in our children or their ability to make the right decision. Our hope remains in our God who is able, who loves them even more than we do, and who loves them with an uncommon love in our world today—a love that always desires their best. Pray for your child in accordance with these truths. Remember— and never forget—the battle is the Lord's; trust Him, obey Him, get out of His way, and stand firm in your hope and faith *in Him*—and He will do the rest! Remember: as long as there is life, there is hope, and "*no word from God will ever fail*" (Luke 1:37). Hold onto what is true regardless of the visible circumstances, and remember that God is always working, even when we don't see evidence of it. He will never leave or forsake your child or you in this battle (Deuteronomy 31:8).

Discussion Questions

1. How hopeful are you that your child will be delivered from or come out of homosexuality? Explain.

2. Do you believe a life based on sin can truly satisfy? Why or why not?

3. What are the biggest threats to your hope? How can you combat them?

4. What costs do you recognize in your own experience where hope is concerned?

5. Upon what (or whom) is your hopefulness based? Why is holding onto hope important?

6. Have you encountered stories of people who have come out of homosexuality? Please share.

7. Does it strengthen your hope to be reminded that nothing is impossible with God? (Luke 18:27) Explain.

8. How does the concept that this visible world is temporary, but the spiritual world (the *in*visible) has eternal impact, affect your perspective of your child's SSA/homosexual lifestyle? (2 Corinthians 4: 18)

9. Second Corinthians 4:2 gives specific instructions about how to handle issues of this world. What are those principles? How can you apply these principles to your relationship with your SSA child?

10. The issue of free will versus God's sovereignty is a tricky one. Can you think of instances in your own life when your free will may have bumped up against God's sovereignty? If our free will overpowered God's sovereignty, would He truly be sovereign? Discuss.

11. Your takeaway: If you were to sum up the impact of this week's lesson in one concise thought, what would that be?

12. Do you have any prayer requests pertaining to your child's SSA you would like to share?

Closing Prayer

Father God,

Holding onto hope is so vital to continuing on this journey with our SSA children, and yet, sometimes, our hope is so fragile! Remind us in those moments, Father, that You are God, You are good, You have our child's best interests at heart, and You are working even when we cannot see the evidence. Remind us that because sin can never satisfy in the long run, and You hate sin, You are working in her life to deliver her out of this sinful lifestyle. Help us also to remember that this sin is born out of painful wounds so we never forget to be compassionate toward our children. You truly do know what our children need and what we need every moment on this journey, Father. Thank You that You see, You know, You understand, and You are faithful even when we are not. Thank You that You will never leave or forsake our children or us. Renew our hope day-by-day. Increase our faith to the measure of the day's difficulty. And help us to remember that, no matter what, You are always good, kind, loving, patient, and full of grace and mercy. This battle is Yours—and You never leave a story without a victorious ending.

In the Mighty Name of Jesus,

Amen.

Chapter Ten
Strategies for Finishing Strong

"Therefore, since we are surrounded by such a great cloud of witnesses, let us throw off everything that hinders and the sin that so easily entangles. And let us run with perseverance the race marked out for us, fixing our eyes on Jesus, the pioneer and perfecter of faith. For the joy set before him he endured the cross, scorning its shame, and sat down at the right hand of the throne of God. Consider him who endured such opposition from sinners, so that you will not grow weary and lose heart."

Hebrews 12:1-3

❧☙

"We may have losses and fail from time to time…but we must have this attitude: one lost battle does not equal the loss of the entire war. The only failure is the man or woman who falls and simply decides to not get back up. A victor just keeps getting back up and heading for the finish line: toward Jesus!"

Dennis Jernigan, *Renewing Your Mind*[20]

er message was clear: I don't want you in my life.

The words shattered my heart into a million pieces. We had

come to an impasse: the place where her new identity came crashing into my identity. Our faith, values, and worldviews were polar opposite. Neither of us could or would compromise. We loved each other still, but the recent conversation had caused us to turn a corner in our relationship. She was devastated by my inability to celebrate her new life, the new love she had found, and their potential wedding. I was devastated by how my inability to compromise my faith and values wounded her. This single event had ushered unspeakable pain and loss into our lives.

So what *do* we do when the inevitable happens? When our SSA son or daughter nails us to the wall and asks: *Can you get on board with my new life or not?* Of course the question may be asked in a million different ways. *Will you come to our wedding? Will you celebrate our new life together? Will you accept this woman as my wife? Will you treat my husband as your son-in-law? Will you be happy that we are adopting a child together? Will you embrace my lifestyle?* The real question behind them all is: *Will you accept me as I am?*

The acceptance your child is seeking in that moment is not a casual one. It is one with a much deeper meaning: *Will you approve of my choices, my lifestyle, my sin? Will you approve of me?*

Everything we've talked about in this Bible study has centered around our adherence to our faith and values within the context of who we are in Christ, obedience to God, and agape love for our children. We have called it compassion without compromise. Acceptance without approval. However, when these questions are posed, those words may sound hollow, for the reality is that this is your child standing before you, asking, expecting, pleading for unconditional acceptance of something that goes against the very foundational core of who we are as children of the Most High God.

In that moment, your heart will leap. Your stomach will churn. Your mind will race. It may feel as though time and eternity pause, as God Himself silences all of heaven as He bends down to hear your response (Psalm 17:6, NLT).

What will you say? How will you respond?

You can offer generalities. *You know I love you with my whole heart, Ryan. You know I want you to be happy, and I want the best for you.*

Trust me when I say, Ryan will not be satisfied with that response.

I need time to think about this, Becca. Can you give me some time to think it through? Becca will most likely be hurt that you even had to think about it! Her response may be: *I'm your daughter! How can you even consider not coming to my wedding?*

The fallout is likely to be even worse if you give a more direct answer: "*I love you, Alex, but I can never condone same-sex marriage. I believe that is not in your best interest, and it is clearly in opposition to God's Word and His will for you. To celebrate such a thing would be to betray my identity in Christ. I'm sorry if that hurts you.*"

In that moment, your relationship with your SSA child may take a very bad turn.

Strategies for Surviving the Confrontation

The first thing to note in this discussion is that your confrontation will most likely look completely different than those listed in this chapter. Your child may be more understanding. Your daughter might not even invite you to her civil union. Your son may not care if you accept his lifestyle or not. And there are a thousand other scenarios that could play out. So first and foremost, *consider your child, her temperament, your journey together thus far, and most of all, your relationship.*

Secondly, try to *anticipate the confrontation.* Have your daughter and her partner been together for a long time? Does their relationship seem to be getting more serious? Prepare as much as possible for the inevitable confrontation. Go to God's Word for wisdom; seek wise counsel from a trusted Christian leader, counselor, or professional life coach; weigh the implications of your response. Essential to preparation is praying for God to give you the words with which to respond. Ask Him to put a guard over your mouth, to fill your mouth with His words, and to nudge you if you are about to say something in opposition to His heart. Measure your words carefully. Generalize if you can, and if you can't, **affirm** your love, **admit** that this is challenging for you, and **ask** for time to work through it before giving an answer.

If appropriate, let her know you've never been faced with something like this before and your desire is to get it right.

The next vital aspect of facing this confrontation is to *lower your expectations*. Do not expect that because the two of you have always been close she will simply accept your response without being hurt or offended. In fact, the closer you have been in your relationship, the harder it will likely be for her to receive a negative response. Do not expect that she will simply say "okay" and then go along as though nothing happened. On the contrary, expect that this confrontation may change the course of your relationship with your child.

Remember the lesson on spiritual warfare? The third imperative for effectively handling a confrontation with your daughter is to *put on the full armor of God (and do so daily)*. This battle is likely to heat up quickly. The enemy will do everything he can to stir up feelings of rejection, hurt, anger, and anything else that might be useful in damaging your relationship with her. Pray and pray hard, especially if the conversation goes sideways.

Next, if your child responds with intense anger and deep hurt, *apologize for what you can*, while remaining true to your identity, faith, and values in Christ. Also, remember if your son is deeply embedded in the world of homosexuality, he may be strongly supported by the ideology of the homosexual community. This community expects Christians to reject their SSA child. Your child will most likely be hoping you aren't one of "those" parents, but if you hold to your faith, he will likely fall back on the rhetoric and biases of the LGBT community. A word to the wise, however; <u>do not</u> *speak to that element of his thinking*. You cannot win that argument, and doing so may very well widen the chasm between your son and you.

Remember also that your child is not the enemy. Your daughter is wounded, and she is most likely deeply in love with her partner. Her perspective is further clouded by these intense feelings of love and happiness. If she is forced to choose between you and her partner, she will almost assuredly choose her partner. Fight the true enemy, but without warring with your daughter.

As you seek to work through the fallout of a confrontation, *remain calm, loving, and supportive in your communication*, but know that *this is the place where your commitment to stand firm in your identity, faith, and values* <u>will be tested</u>. Will you remain strong in your commitment or will you give in to the pressure to embrace your son's sin? The former may result in the loss of the relationship with him for a time; the latter may serve to further solidify his homosexual identity. Remaining strong in your faith may cause more hurt between your son and you; it may cause him to distance himself from you and move more intensely toward his partner; likewise, it may also be a catalyst God eventually uses to set him free from that life. In addition to solidifying his homosexual identity, giving in to the request to condone his lifestyle may also cause a dissonance in your relationship with God, and it may prolong your son's foray into the gay lifestyle.

Remember: obedience to God is cooperation with God; obedience to the flesh is rebellion against God (Luke 11:23). Neither path is easy. Nothing about this journey is easy! But as we cooperate with God, He will see us through the hardships and heartaches, and He will continue to work in the hearts and minds of our children according to His timing, plans, and purposes for them. We cannot prevent God's plans through our disobedience, but we can work in opposition to Him. When all is said and done, which do you want to be your legacy? Live your life in the details, but always with the big picture in mind. Roll with the punches, but never lose sight of the end goal. Choose to cooperate with God.

The final strategy is to *renew your mind*. Renewing your mind is simply telling yourself the truth—based on God's character and His Word, by the power of His Spirit—regardless of the circumstances. When we have been in this kind of confrontation, our thoughts and emotions will run roughshod over us if we aren't careful. (The enemy loves when we let that happen!) Be intentional about your thoughts as you process the consequences of your stance whether you stood strong or gave in.

If you stood strong in your commitment to your faith and identity in Christ, the fallout may be excruciating. Your child may have cussed you out or told you he no longer wants anything to do with you—or any number of other hurtful things. As his words reverberate in your head and heart, the temptations will come flying at you...temptations to renege on your stance, to blame God for allowing this to happen, to lose hope and fall headlong into despair, or even to despair of life. If the holidays are coming, your heart may be especially heavy. Holidays are for family, and the thought of setting one fewer place at the table for Christmas may be crushing. At moments like these, it is absolutely crucial to recognize what you are thinking and feeling, call them what they are, and then tell yourself the truth according to God's character and Word. Remember, the enemy is the father of lies; he is the deceiver and his M.O. is to speak just enough truth to sound valid while twisting it up enough that truth is completely squeezed out of it. This is deception at its finest, and he's really good at what he does.

But we don't have to fall prey to his schemes or his lies. We have the truth at our fingertips. God's Word is true, His way is right, and His promises are sure. He promises to never leave us or forsake us (Deuteronomy 31:6), to hold us by His righteous right hand (Isaiah 41:10), to take what the enemy means for evil and bring good from it (Genesis 50:20); He promises to carry onto completion the good work He has begun in us and in our children (Philippians 1:6). As we remember and rehearse His truths, the lies of the enemy fall away. Our despair turns to hope. Our sadness turns to joy. His light pierces the darkness of our hearts and minds and—even in the worst circumstances—that light will shine through us. The result is that the enemy's schemes are frustrated, and even in the pain, God will bring about good things.

Renewing your mind is about replacing your thoughts and the lies of the enemy with the mind of Christ—the very same one who, for the joy set before Him, endured our cross. *We* are His joy! *Our children* are His joy! *Our trusting in Him when everything in our world speaks to the contrary* brings Him joy. Knowing that we want to partner with Him to bless our children brings Him joy, especially when we are making that choice in the midst of great sacrifice and suffering. Just as praising Him in the storm fills Him with joy, so does our willingness to stand firm in our faith when we are experiencing great pain and loss. We cannot see or know what the future holds, but as the saying goes, we know Who holds the future! We know that as we stand firm in our faith in Jesus, we never stand alone.

Be advised, however, that we may have to hold this position for a long time. As a result, we may lose our relationship with our kids for a time. But God rewards our faithfulness in countless ways, and He will sustain us no matter what! Trust Him. Praise Him. Believe Him. He's got you. He's got them. He's got this. Remember it. Rehearse it. Count on it. He will sustain you as you renew your mind with His truth.

Mending the Relationship

We hope we never have one of those divisive confrontations with our SSA children, but the reality is almost sure that, at some point, your child will seek some level of affirmation or acceptance of his lifestyle from you that conflicts with your faith and values. If you take the compassion without compromise approach, it is likely that her feelings will be hurt and your relationship may be injured.

If this happens, and even if you did and said everything "right," there will likely be reparations to make. Following are some things to reflect and act upon as the Holy Spirit leads you.

1. Write down the more prominent statements she made, beginning with her plea, request, or expectation. Consider what may have been behind her words. Was she looking for acceptance? Affirmation of her lifestyle? Something else? You can't know for certain, but it is always advisable to consider what someone may be trying to communicate. Often, during such conversations, the emotions of all parties involved—and sometimes the words themselves—get in the way. Consider what she may have meant, rather than simply what she said. (Engage in healthy detachment!)

2. Process the conversation with an objective person who understands these dynamics (e.g. your counselor, therapist, pastor, or professional life coach). Ask for their insights from the perspective of seeking to understand your child rather than having your feelings understood or defending your position. Approach this process with humility and a desire to repair the relationship, not to be right.

3. Pray and ask God to give you discernment. Ask Him to convict you of anything hurtful or damaging you may have said or done within the context of your relationship with your son or daughter, and especially during the confrontation. If He convicts you of something, own it, admit it, and make the commitment to abandon that viewpoint/action/etc. in the future. Ask Him to forgive you; accept His forgiveness; and then release yourself from self-condemnation.

4. When the time is right, admit your sin/error to your child. Let him know how sorry you are for how your words or attitudes may have hurt him, but *do so without apologizing for remaining true to your identity in Christ.* (Don't even speak to the issues that caused the discord, at this time!) Do not defend yourself in any way. Then ask for his forgiveness as well. Don't expect immediate forgiveness. Give him time to work through his feelings as well as your apology.

5. Ask her if there is anything else you said or did that hurt her. If she shares some things with you, apologize for the pain you caused. Let her know how much you hate that your words or actions hurt or offended her. Reaffirm your love for her and let her know how much her heart and your relationship with her means to you.

6. Let him know you would like to talk further about the issues when the time is right. Tell him you want to hear him better, to understand his perspectives and his needs, and that you will strive to do so. Let him know his heart, feelings, and needs matter to you. Tell him you care for him and his partner (if you sincerely mean it), and that your relationship with him/them matters significantly to you. (Yes, I'm repeating myself—because this aspect of the conversation is vital!) Let him know that even if your perspectives differ, you will always love him and want a relationship with him.

7. Whenever you do speak again about the issues at hand, focus on the heart of the matter, the expressed or implied needs she shares with you. If an impasse remains, ask if you might

agree to disagree while still maintaining a mutually loving and respectful relationship. Let her know you are in no way rejecting her because of her identity, and ask her also to not reject you because of yours.

8. Strive to maintain a calm, caring, respectful, and humble tone. If things begin to heat up again, ask for time to consider his words. Let him know again how much it means to you to get this right, and that you are willing to fight for your relationship—<u>not</u> for your ideology. <u>Leave God, faith, sin, etc. out of the conversation</u>*!*

Approach your son or daughter with love, humility, love, compassion, love, respect, and more love. Determine to see him as God sees him—as a dearly beloved child who is wounded and hurting, and with a desire for relationship above that of being right. As we've seen previously in this Bible study, Jesus never forced His views on others. He never beat them over the head with their sin or His righteousness. He treated each individual (sinner) with an overabundance of love with the desired end goal in mind. He never forced the issue in the moment, but gave people time to let His love work on them. We must follow His example.

Even if you follow all these suggestions, the possibility remains that your relationship with your daughter may be damaged beyond immediate repair. Affirm your love and respect for her; give her time and space if that is what she needs or asks for. Then press into God with all your heart. Such a division will hurt both your daughter and you, but trust that God has not abandoned either of you. He is still working even when we see no evidence of that. Trust His heart, His plan, and His timing, and continue to stand in the gap for her. Praise God in this "storm." Resist the lies of the enemy about the situation. Renew your mind and reaffirm your commitment to honor God with your life—and with your pain. This season will not be easy, but He will sustain you.

Reach out to your son periodically with a text, phone message, or note to let him know you love and miss him, and that you hope all is well with him. Keep the doors of communication open to whatever degree he will allow, always respecting his wishes and/or boundaries. But ultimately, leave the relationship in God's hands and trust His plans for your child and you. He is trustworthy. Never give up hope for reconciliation of the relationship or that He will rescue your son from the homosexual lifestyle. Remember, as long as there is life, there is hope in Christ Jesus!

Healing Begins with Me

Over the course of this study we have determined that Same-Sex Attraction is, at its simplest, the result of deep wounds in our child's heart. For that reason, SSA is not simply our child's issue—it's a *family* issue. Not only does SSA affect our entire family, it is often within the family environment that SSA has found its way into our child's life. Please hear me: *this is not about placing blame on you or any member of your family*. We are all broken, hurting people with deep wounds of our own, and for most of us, we have not experienced healing for all or even most of our own wounds. The result is that, when we are wounded, we tend to operate out of those broken places, which leads to hurt within our relationships.

What does that mean? Can we go back and undo what has been done in the past? No, of course not, but we can work to find healing within ourselves now. At the end of the day, healing for our SSA child and for our family begins with the person looking back at you in the mirror each morning. Healing begins with you.

Now I must caution you, the healing process is often a painful one. It requires getting honest with ourselves about hurts or wounds or failures we may have been working very hard to ignore for decades. It means bringing those buried wounds out into the light and leaving them there until they no longer have power over us.

There's a common axiom in counseling circles: *The power is in the secret.* Whatever we push down, ignore, or deny has a powerful effect on us. Sometimes we have to work hard to keep those things hidden and buried, which can be exhausting. Sometimes we're not even aware of them! Whatever the case, the infection of those wounds begins to seep out into other areas of your life in ways you may not even be aware of or notice. Once that secret is revealed and laid bare, its power over you is exponentially diminished. Secrecy feeds shame and deception. Bringing those secrets into the light—especially with an emotionally healthy and trusted friend or professional—drains away the shame, exposing the lies you've believed, and allowing healing to begin.

While I encourage you to seek professional help, there are some steps you can take on your own to begin to heal. A word of caution, however: bringing those old wounds out into the light is a little like having major surgery. It's going to hurt *more* before you begin to feel better. The beauty of awareness is that you will know where the pain is coming from and that it is part of the healing process, whereas the cause of the pain you have felt to this point may have been hidden. Like the monsters in your closet or under your bed when you were a child, the things that scare us the most nearly always look smaller and less fierce when you bring them out into the light of day.

The first step in beginning to heal is always prayer. Ask God to bring the things to light that need healing, and to give you everything you need as you do so. Ask Him to protect you from schemes or attacks of the enemy. Ask Him to surround you with both His ministering angels and His warring angels (Hebrews 1:13-14; 2 Chronicles 32: 20-22).

Second, write out the things God brings to your mind in a journal designated for this healing process. As you write those things, you are shattering the hidden power of the secrets you have buried for so long. Journal about the experiences that caused those hurts, the messages you received as a result of those experiences, and the feelings those messages planted in your heart. Often, the enemy will take every opportunity—even from our earliest years—to plant messages in our hearts about who we are based on how others treat us. Then, once the seeds of those messages take root, they become the filter through which we view how other people treat us as we grow up and even into adulthood. Identifying those messages is key.

Third, the only thing that will defeat a lie (or deceptive message) is the truth. Make a list of those messages, then go to God's Word and find what He says about you in those same areas. For example, if you grew up feeling unworthy of being loved, what does God say about you? Psalm 139 is a beautiful example of how much God loves you! Write God's truth next to each lie.

Finally, repent (turn away) from having believed these lies; reject each one, one-by-one, choosing to believe God instead. Ask Him to show you how those lies affected your behaviors and attitudes—especially those that may have contributed to the dysfunctional environment in your (secondary) home and family. Ask Him to completely heal those areas of your life. Thank God for showing you the truth, and ask Him to embed those truths into your heart, mind, and spirit. Ask Him to remind you of them often, and to make you aware of those times when you are tempted to pick up the lies again. Create reminders of your own; place them on your bathroom mirror; write them on notecards to carry in your purse or wallet. Put a daily reminder in your phone with a list of these truths. Choose, each time you read them, to believe them, and thank God for replacing the lies with His truth. This is the process of renewing your mind. It is replacing the lies of the enemy with God's truth.

While this process is a detailed plan of action, it is not a quick fix. The lies you have believed all your life have created deep grooves in your mind, and it can take a long time to fill in those grooves by creating new ones. Give yourself grace—and time—for this process. Determine to stick with it until those old lies and buried secrets no longer have any power over you.

As you begin to heal, your attitudes and behaviors with your family will begin to change. You will have set into motion a ripple effect in your family. Everything we do puts something in motion. As we begin to heal, our words, actions, and attitudes—even our very demeanor will begin to change. As a result, our relationships may be strengthened. Trust may be rebuilt. Your home environment may begin to change. As God begins to heal you, He may very likely begin a ripple effect of healing in your family.

God loves you and your family. He has great things in store for you. Your healing, by virtue of His mercy and grace, is only the beginning. Determine today to let your family's healing begin with you.

DIGGING DEEPER: Journal Questions

1. Have you blown it big time with your SSA child? What could you have done differently?

2. If you have blown it, were you able to make things right? If not, is there something you can do to that end?

3. If you've blown it, did you apologize and ask for forgiveness? Did you ask God to forgive you? Have you been able to accept His forgiveness and to forgive yourself? Why or why not? What is the difference between God's forgiveness and the forgiveness we offer to one another and/or to ourselves?

   a. God's forgiveness (1 John 2:1-3):
   b. Our forgiveness (Colossians 3:13):

4. Are there things you would like to say to your SSA child that you can't or shouldn't? Write them out in your journal as a way of processing them, but not to share with your child.

5. Do you have fears about the time when you may yet be faced with a confrontation? What can you do on this side of it to prepare?

6. Write out a prayer in your journal asking God to give you His wisdom, insight, and discernment in preparation for any confrontations to come. Release your fears to Him. Ask Him to prepare your heart and mind and that of your child.

7. Reread the last section of this chapter: Healing Begins with Me. How do you feel about beginning that process? Ask God to speak to you specifically about where you need healing.

DEEPER STILL: Study Questions

1. Read Hebrews 12:1-3. What was the joy set before Christ that helped Him endure the cross? How do we "fix our eyes on Jesus?"

2. Also in Hebrews 12:1-3, what is the key to not growing weary and losing heart? What does it mean to "consider Him…?" Write your answers out on a note to place where you can see it daily or carry it with you.

3. Blowing it with your SSA child may certainly cause you to feel like a failure. Read Proverbs 24:16a. According to this verse, what constitutes being a "failure?" Do you agree with that definition? Why or why not? Can you accept that we all make mistakes and blow it sometimes, and doing so is merely a result of being human?

4. Are your expectations still in need of adjustment? What is the difference between expectations and hope? How do you let go of expectations without losing heart?

   a. 2 Corinthians 4:15-17

   b. Hebrews 12:1-4

5. Do you need to forgive your child for anything? Are you willing to do that? When you choose to forgive him, do you need to tell him so? Why or why not?

6. What does Romans 12:9 say about love? If your response to your child's confrontation deeply wounded her, what can you own, and for what can you sincerely apologize—without compromising your faith? Write out an example of such an apology.

7. Imagine for a moment your relationship with your SSA child is a play. Describe each of the characters according to the role they are playing and what the possible root issue or desire may be. What does Romans 8:31-37 have to say in this regard?

    a. Your child:

    b. You:

    c. God:

    d. Satan:

    e. Is there a victim? Victor? Vanquisher? Villain?

8. Read James 1:2-8, 12. According to this passage, how should we view these trials with our SSA kids?

    _____

    _____

    _____

Make a list of the do's and don'ts. What are the benefits of handling our trials in this manner?

Do:	Don't:

Benefits:

_____

_____

_____

9. Read the following passages of Scripture. What does each one say about your mind? What do they say about our responsibility within the context of relationships with others?

    a.   Ephesians 4:22-32

    b.   Romans 12:2

    c.   2 Corinthians 10:5

    d.   1 Corinthians 2:16

10. Read Romans 15:4-6 (NIV). What does it mean to have "the mind of Christ?" Why is that important?

11. Read the following Scriptures and write out the main point of each. What do these verses mean in regard to finishing strong with your SSA child?

   a.   Matthew 26:41

   b.   2 Corinthians 12:9

   c.   Romans 5:5

   d.   Isaiah 49:23b

   e.   Romans 12:18

12. If your relationship with your child is broken, how do you hold onto hope in the midst of your grief? Write out your plan of action.

13. Has God revealed any areas of your life that need heal-ing—especially in areas that impact your SSA child? Do you believe God can heal those wounds? Why or why not?

14. Read the following verses and write the main idea in each:

   a.   Psalm 147:3

    b.   Isaiah 61:1-4

    c.   Matthew 4:23

15. Do you want to be healed? Read Matthew 20:31-34. If Jesus asked this question of you, how would you respond? Are you willing to do whatever it takes? What, if anything, is holding you back?

APPLICATION: Write out your takeaway.

_____

_____

_____

_____

_____

_____

_____

_____

_____

_____

_____

_____

Strategies for Finishing Strong

*"Therefore, since we are surrounded by such a great
cloud of witnesses, let us throw off everything that
hinders and the sin that so easily entangles. And let us
run with perseverance the race marked out for us, fixing
our eyes on Jesus, the pioneer and perfecter of faith. For
the joy set before him he endured the cross, scorning its
shame, and sat down at the right hand of the throne of
God. Consider him who endured such opposition from
sinners, so that you will not grow weary and lose heart."*

Hebrews 12:1-3

§☙

*"We may have losses and fail from time to time…but we must
have this attitude: one lost battle does not equal the loss of the
entire war. The only failure is the man or woman who falls and
simply decides to not get back up. A victor just keeps getting
back up and heading for the finish line: toward Jesus!"*

Dennis Jernigan, *Renewing Your Mind*[20]

One of the great deceptions of our society today is the idea that if our
views on political, ideological, religious, or cultural issues differ,
we cannot be in relationship. While these differences can indeed create

a high degree of stress in a relationship, differences alone do not determine our ability to have strong, healthy, and close relationships with each other. This is especially true where our families are concerned.

The determining factors of healthy relationships have nothing at all to do with our views, ideologies, etc. Instead, *the essential elements for any close relationship are respect, healthy boundaries, kindness, consideration, and forgiveness, all within a context of sincere love.* Each person bears both the image of God and autonomy. That autonomy means each individual has the right to determine what is important to them, how they will live their life, what they believe, and how they will respond to the situations and circumstances they face. Because you raised your children in a Christian home does not make them Christians. (Or if you didn't, it doesn't mean they won't become Christians!) Because you are a registered Democrat or Republican doesn't mean they must be also. As adults, their beliefs, values, and ideologies are their own to determine, define, and adopt.

As are ours.

Each of us is on our own individual journey through this life. Each one chooses where to go, how to get there, and who to do life with along the way. Of course, it is human nature to surround ourselves with people who agree with our views. However, the family structure is not one of choice, but of design. The family you have was God's design for you. It may be one of blessing, encouragement, safety, and unconditional love, or it may be one of conflict, testing, trials, and hurt, or any combination of the two. But one thing is certain: we do not treat family with the same *laissez-faire* attitude with which we treat changing jobs or even friendships. Jobs and friends come and go, but family is a lifelong institution constructed by God Himself.

Does that mean family is more important than everything else? No, of course not. Some families are toxic and all the healthy boundaries, forgiveness, and kindness may not redeem those relationships. However, even when there is a level of toxicity, God may call us to retain some relationship with our family. (That is another discussion for another time!)

The point is that family is important because God created it, ordained it, and because He values it highly. Our job is to maintain a healthy family unit *as far as it depends on us*, and that does not mean we have to agree on everything! In fact, the only values we must agree on are respect and sincere love (which includes kindness, consideration, and forgiveness) within the constraints of healthy boundaries. Everything else is optional. Faith and religion, political leanings, and personal life choices fall under the umbrella of autonomy. Your adult children have the right to define who they are and what they believe, as do you. When their choices and ours are on opposite ends of the spectrum, it is mutual respect and sincere love within healthy boundaries that enable us to continue to enjoy close and mutually satisfying relationships with one another.

When culture defines the boundaries of our relationships, we all lose. And while your SSA son or daughter will have to make the choice of whether to follow culture's definition of family or the one outlined here, it is certainly a conversation worth having. We cannot force them to see even this issue as we do, but we can exemplify it in our choices, behaviors, words, and attitudes. And we can pray for God to redeem our families for His glory and purposes, according to His will.

Once we've had this conversation, our part is to do the right thing in obedience to God, and to surrender our hopes, expectations, and perceived rights to Him. As we do so in an attitude of obedience and trust, we can let go of the outcomes. It doesn't mean doing so won't hurt; but never forget that God enters our pain with us, and He will always see us through. What's more, He is the only one who can change the hearts and minds of our children. As we continue to stand in the gap for them, we are doing our part. We can trust Him to do His. His promises are true.

Discussion Questions

1. Have you had a conflict or confrontation with your SSA child that has gone sideways? How did you handle the situation? Do you need to make amends? What would that look like?

2. How do you apologize for hurting someone without apologizing for your faith and values? Is it possible to do so? What are the implications?

3. Do you need to forgive your child for anything related to his SSA? Does forgiving him require having a discussion with him? Why or why not?

4. What parts of your relationship with your SSA child depend on you? On him or her?

5. What does it mean to finish strong?

6. If you have had a major confrontation with your child that resulted in a division in your relationship, how can you endure to the end? How can you finish strong? (If you haven't yet had such a confrontation, imagine that your child has severed her relationship with you and answer the questions posed above.) Where is God in this situation? Discuss.

7. Which of the questions answered this week helped to clarify your thinking on those topics? Explain.

8. What does the phrase "healing begins with me" mean? Do you recognize areas in your own life that need healing? Is there anything stopping you from beginning that process?

9. Which of the questions answered this week helped to clarify your thinking on those topics? Explain.

10. Your takeaway: If you were to sum up the impact of this week's lesson in one concise thought, what would that be?

11. Do you have any prayer requests pertaining to your child's SSA you would like to share?

Closing Prayer

Father God,

Our hearts hurt when we think about or experience conflict with our SSA children. Our natural instinct is to 'fix' the problem—to do whatever it takes to make the pain go away and to repair the rift in our relationship. But You have called us to a higher calling: to lay down our lives to You—for Your purposes, for Your glory in us, and in our relationships with our children. We want to obey You, Father, but though our spirits are willing, our flesh is weak. Strengthen us by Your Spirit! As we renew our minds, give us the mind of Christ. Give us Your hope that does not disappoint and the strength to finish strong. And may our children return to You and to who You have created them to be, according to Your will and timing.

In the Mighty Name of Jesus,

Amen

Conclusion

WHERE DO YOU GO FROM HERE®

We've come a long way in our ten-week journey together. The question now is, *where do you go from here?* If your group is disbanding as this Bible study ends, you may want to consider starting your own home-based support group that continues to meet weekly, bi-monthly, monthly—or whatever time frame works for your group members. You have already traveled this far together; continuing the group in someone's home provides for ongoing support for those who need it. (If you would like suggestions or help in starting or facilitating support group meetings at home, please send an email to Uncommon Love Ministries at <u>uncommonloveonline@gmail.com</u>.) Whether you are just getting started on this journey or you've been in it for decades, the support of others who are also going through something similar and who understand is invaluable. I encourage you to keep the connections you have.

Another option for moving forward is to consider facilitating one of these Bible studies yourself, either at your church or at another church in your area. Besides being supportive, this Bible study is also intended to educate Christian parents and others about this very difficult issue of SSA and homosexuality. As our culture continues to embrace homosexuality as normal, more and more people are going to be coming out, meaning that more and more families are going to need help, information, and support. Now that you know what you know, consider sharing with others like you who need to know as well. Uncommon Love Ministries has a facilitator's guide and training available for those interested in facilitating a Bible study group.

You might also consider approaching your church leaders to ask them about hosting a Raising Awareness Event that is open to your community. Many churches are too afraid to speak out publicly about the issue of SSA and homosexuality, leaving a majority of the population of Christian parents unaware of what to do or where to turn. Having one of these community events is an excellent way to let other people in your community know there is help available to them at your church. We at Uncommon Love Ministries would consider it an honor to come to your church to facilitate such an event. There is no need to reinvent the wheel! Our passion is educating, informing, and supporting Christian parents about this challenging and life-changing issue.

Also, please write to us and share your success stories with us! We want to know how God is working in your child's life and in your life!

However you go forward, do so knowing that God is with you on your journey. He is with your child, and He will never leave nor forsake either of you! Whatever you need today, can be found in Him. Trust Him with the life of your child and with your own life. He is faithful to carry out His promises, and best of all, He is still in the business of doing the impossible! He is the God who softens hearts, renews minds, and transforms lives. May He bless you beyond all you could ask or imagine in Jesus!

In the grip of His unfailing love and grace,
Mary Comm & the Uncommon Love Team

APPENDIX

Answers to Common Questions

As the parents of SSA children, you either have been or will be faced with a number of scenarios about which you will be required to make difficult decisions. These decisions will affect your relationship with your child and others. Discovering the right or best answers in those situations can be daunting, and you will no doubt receive strong opinions from those around you. Often, however, the opinions of the people in your circles of influence may be tainted by a number of factors: their political perspective, their perspective from a humanistic worldview, their perspective from a Biblical but legalistic bent, a balanced Biblical perspective, or personal experience with a similar scenario—either their own or the story of someone close to them. Whatever the case, you will get every answer under the sun when you ask for people's advice, and sometimes even when you don't!

What you have to decide from this moment forward is: *What is the source of wisdom I most value and respect, and what sources should I set aside?* When you are able to make this determination, the cacophony of voices in your life will cause you less stress and angst. And when those difficult, unforeseen situations arise, you will be better equipped to handle them.

Your second decision is the manner in which you respond when faced with a situation you have not previously considered. In these moments, the best response is to respectfully and lovingly ask for time to explore the question at hand.

For example, if your SSA child asks you a question concerning your position on something you have not previously considered, a good response may be, *"I've not thought about that before. Could you give me some time to think about it, and I will get back to you?"* This response lets your child know you care about her enough to give it some thought, and that you care enough about her feelings not to give a knee-jerk response. There is always wisdom in asking permission to take time to think through the question at hand. Then, when the time comes to consider the question, do so thoughtfully, prayerfully, and with a willingness to respond in accordance to God's will—not what may be the path of least resistance with your child. Seek to please God first; He will take care of the rest.

With that said, following are a number of common questions parents of SSA children encounter. This list is not comprehensive, but hopefully, it will give you good examples of how to think through similar issues. Please know, our purpose here is not to tell you what decisions you should make or boundaries you should set regarding your SSA son or daughter. Those decisions are between you and God. The following section is merely a guideline with suggestions.

Answers to Common Questions

Q. *How do I accept my child where she is without compromising my Christian beliefs?*

A. Of all the questions Christian parents ask, this one is perhaps the hardest to answer. It helps to remain aware that, as followers of Christ, we are Christians *first* and parents *second* (Luke 14:25-26). Further, keeping in mind that your child's SSA is the result of deep heart wounds, helps to maintain a sense of compassion for what she is experiencing, along with a deep desire for her to be healed. (Job 2:7-10; Matthew 15:19)

Another important aspect is to remember that your child's sin is between him and Christ (Psalm 51:4). At its very deepest point, his sin is not about you; it is the result of wounding and deception regarding his identity, God's character, etc.

However, when he displays his sin openly in front of you, you have to decide how or if you should respond. If you choose in that moment to alleviate his discomfort, you have moved from compassion to compromise. Ultimately, you must leave his choice to sin in God's hands. However, you should not attempt to make him feel comfortable in his sin. God often uses our discomfort in our sin to convict us and bring godly sorrow that leads to repentance (2 Corinthians 7:10). If you do what you can to remove that discomfort, you are rescuing your child from one of the consequences of his choice. Even more, it means you have then compromised your faith.

Now, does that mean we should preach a sermon every time we witness a sinful act? No, of course not! In fact, we must remember that everyone—ourselves included—reacts (more often than not) with opposition to those who point out our sin (Nehemiah 9:29). This means when we do confront an act of sin, we need to pray about how to handle the situation first, and then we must do so with an abundance of love, compassion, and humility. Finally, we should be prepared for any backlash.

Before a situation arises, however, it is best to decide where your boundary lies between compassion and compromise, acceptance and approval. For example, in order to be loving toward your child and his partner, you may schedule a dinner out at a restaurant with the two of them, but you may not want to allow them into your home together. What's the difference? The first is on neutral ground; the second is your home—an extension of who you are and of what your values are. Or if you invite them into your home, your boundary may be one of respect in regard to not showing affection (PDA) for one another in your home. Only you and your spouse can determine where your boundaries lie.

For example, you might ask her, in a very loving, compassionate way, *"What is your perspective of my stance on your relationship with (name of partner)? If she says, "I know you don't agree with it, Mom,"* then respond, with *"Thank you.... That's right. So would you please respect me by not openly showing affection to your partner in front of me? I love you and respect your choices; I am just really uncomfortable seeing those behaviors."* Or, if she responds to your question with, *"You seem to be coming around to the idea of my sexual identity,"* you may respond—again, with all the love and compassion you can communicate—by saying, *"I'm sorry if I gave you the impression that I'm okay with your being gay. You know that I love you with all my heart, and while I respect your choices, I am really uncomfortable seeing those behaviors."* She may become very angry with you at such a statement. She may even sever her relationship with you for a time.

What you have to decide—beforehand—is, are you willing to stand firm in your faith and identity in Christ at the risk of your relationship with your child? Or are you willing to compromise your faith in order to alleviate her discomfort? The answer to that question will reveal where your highest priority is. Are you a parent first and a Christian second? Or the other way around? Everything we do has consequences. A choice to stand firm in your faith, with lots of love, compassion, kindness, etc. means the relationship may suffer. However, a choice to compromise your faith in order to alleviate her discomfort may mean she stays in her sin longer. Either way, you are making a statement about your faith. This is a hard truth, but it must be said: *faith that doesn't move you to stand firm isn't very important to you.*

Another truth is, when we refuse to stand firm in our faith and principles on the issue of homosexuality, we give the impression we are okay with homosexuality. Your child's natural assumption, as you begin to accept public displays of affection in your home, is to believe you have moved from acceptance of her decision to affirmation or approval of it. She may begin to think you've come around to the idea.

It is true our job is not to play Holy Spirit by convicting others of their sin; that is His job (John 16:8)! Our job is to be Christ to them while praying for them, which also means we do not openly condone, dismiss, or pretend that sinful behavior doesn't matter to us. Jesus never did that! His example to us was to be loving to those caught in sin, while still maintaining that right living before God is the ultimate goal. This is where the issue of compromise comes in. If/when you strive to make your child feel comfortable in her sin, you have crossed a line from compassion for her wound into compromise. Once we have made our position clear that SSA behavior is sin, showing her unconditional love will provide the best possibility for our relationship with her to be a catalyst for her freedom from this sin, for repentance, and for restoration. Our refusal to compromise our faith communicates to her that we are serious about our faith and belief in Jesus' way of doing things and that His way is best. We must never waver on that!

Therefore, as you maintain a consistent acceptance of your child—of his decisions (if an adult) pertaining to his lifestyle, partner, etc.—and without offering blanket approval of his homosexual behavior, you are offering him a solid, trusting, and close relationship based on your strong faith in Jesus Christ (John 8:1-11). If the opposite occurs, your child may choose to sever the relationship. While that will hurt you both deeply, at least you will be able to rest in the fact that you obeyed Christ. God is faithful when we obey Him—and He can use even division for His purposes. As Scripture says, *"If it is possible, as far as it depends on you, live at peace with everyone"* Romans 12:18. When you choose to do the right thing before God—even if the situation goes very bad—you are entrusting the outcome to Him. Remember, He is trustworthy.

Remember too, that his partner is just as wounded as your child is and needs freedom through Christ just as much as your child does. Just as you would pray for a heterosexual child's partner, pray for and show love to your SSA child's partner. Love builds bridges of trust, healing, and reconciliation. Rejection, shaming, harsh judgment, condemnation, or criticisms cause division.

In the end, how you handle these specific instances is an individual decision *up to the point of sinning against God*. Pray about these issues, surrender your feelings and desires to God along with the outcomes of the situation, and ask Him to give you His heart toward them (Galatians 3:26-27).

Q. *Whom should I tell and when?*

A. Deciding whom to tell about your child's homosexuality and when to do so can be a difficult question as well. It is important to first ask your son's permission to tell others—especially if he has not yet come out publicly. If he does not want you to tell anyone, respectfully let him know that this new revelation is very painful and hard for you and you need support; ask him if he could allow you to tell one or two people whom you know to be trustworthy. Let him know you are hurting, and hopefully, he will grant you permission to tell someone. Give him time to consider your request and then respect his decision.

Once your child gives you permission to tell someone, the second issue to consider is determining who is truly trustworthy to hold this secret in confidence. Is there someone in your life who has repeatedly kept your confidence? The issue of trust is vital in this circumstance. That person should also be someone you hold in high esteem as a mature believer who will point you to Jesus and to God's Word, rather than to the world's perspective of the issue. Trust isn't simply about keeping the secret; it's also about trusting that person to give you godly counsel.

As your child comes out publicly, you will no longer be under any commitments to keep the secret. If she has come out publicly, you are now free to tell whomever about your daughter's SSA. Now the question has to do with anticipating how these people will respond, which is discussed in the next section.

Q. *How do I deal with others who are judgmental, critical, etc., to my child or to me?*

A. In the current climate of our culture, you will no doubt encounter many people who will be openly accepting of your child's SSA identity—even within the church. Others will respond with anything from harsh judgment of your son, to questions about your parenting, to telling you and possibly your child he will burn in hell if he doesn't repent. Others, still, may reject your child and/or you. While people's responses can be very hurtful to you and your son, it is important to remember they will be held accountable by God for their critical, harsh, or condemning statements, as will we all. Remember, their sin is between them and God. When people make these comments, it is okay to simply walk away. Make a mental note that these people are not safe for you. You do not need to set them straight. Honestly, there is probably nothing you could say that would change their minds. However, if you need to say anything, let them know your son is wounded and ask them to pray for him and your family. Pray for God to work in this area of their lives for His glory and choose to forgive them for any hurts they may have caused.

If you're in a solid place of strength, you may want to take that opportunity to educate these gay-affirming people about the root cause of SSA being deep, emotional wounds from your daughter's childhood. Further, because children with SSA tend to be highly sensitive, you can set a boundary with critical people, letting them know you expect your child to be treated with respect, sensitivity, and Christ-like love. If the offending person is unwilling or unable to strive for that, there may be a need to set healthy boundaries in the affected relationships until such an attitude of kindness and respect is established.

If they are willing to be loving and supportive, remember that in their attempts to do so they may make some significant mistakes by saying things that are still offensive. As long as they are trying to be loving, come alongside them in an instructive manner to help them know what things to say or not say. We all make mistakes when this issue is new in our personal lives. Offer grace and patience to those who wish to get it right but stumble along the way.

If your child is within hearing distance of critical comments, voice your unconditional love for him, just as God loves him, affirming that nothing could ever cause your love for your son to be diminished. God demonstrates over and over throughout Scripture that this is how He loves us, and it's how we are called to love one another. Then leave it at that. *Always defend your child without defending the behavior.* Doing so lets him know you always have his back, and he won't soon forget it.

Q. *Will my child be condemned to hell for her homosexual behavior?*

A. The sin of homosexuality is not an unforgivable sin. The only unforgivable sin revealed in Scripture is blaspheming the Holy Spirit (Mark 3:28-29). According to the Blue Letter Bible (https://www.blueletterBible.org), the word *blaspheme* (*blasphemeo*) in Mark 3:29 literally means "to speak evil of, vilify, defame, or revile (insult, abuse, condemn or scorn)" the Holy Spirit. There is no other sin—even the sin of homosexuality—that is unforgivable. However, every sin brings consequences. Jesus paid a high price for our sins, so we should never take sin lightly—not our children's sin, and not our sin. But Scripture says that, when we belong to Him, there is nothing in heaven above or earth below that can separate us from God's love

(Romans 8:35-39). We can rest in the truth of His Word. If your child has genuinely surrendered his life to Christ, you can rest in the assurance of his salvation.

Q. *Does God recognize same-sex marriage?*

A. God's design for marriage and sex throughout the Bible is that which occurs between one man and one woman. Every reference in Scripture related to marriage is between a man and a woman without exception. Further, because there is nothing within the human heart that is new under the sun, we know that sexual sin of every kind has existed since the dawn of mankind. Therefore, those who would presume that God was merely shortsighted when it came to "homosexual love"–that which occurs between two people of the same gender within the constraints of a committed, monogamous relationship— could not be more mistaken.

God spoke this vast, unsearchable universe into being (Genesis 1). His understanding is beyond what we can fathom (Isaiah 40:28). Further, God is unchanging; He remains the same throughout the expanse of time (Hebrews 13:8). He does not change based on how our culture, knowledge, or perspectives change. Therefore, it is extremely arrogant to think God was shortsighted about anything. So, given that marriage is defined in the Bible as being between one man and one woman, it would be a serious stretch of the imagination to think God recognizes or honors same-sex marriage. Homosexuality, as described by Scripture, is "unnatural," the "sinful desire" of a result of "darkened hearts," it is "shameful," "degrading," and it is "a lie" (Romans 1:21-27). It is characterized as "sexual immorality" in the Word of God, therefore, it is sin. It is not God's best for His children, and it is safe to say He does not recognize nor does He honor it as a true marriage.

Q. *Should I attend their same-sex union?*

A. This question is truly a heart-rending one. Every parent looks forward to the day their child gets married with mixed emotion, but by and large, it is a wonderful day of celebration for a family to experience. However, when your child is in a homosexual relationship, the anticipation or news of a wedding can be extremely painful. Indeed, it is a great loss.

No one can tell you the right choice to make in this situation. Scripture does not speak directly to it, however, knowing God's Word and His heart on the topic, there are a few things to take into consideration.

As mentioned earlier, the boundary line between showing compassion and compromising your faith should be the place for you to examine when it comes to deciding whether or not to attend your child's same-sex union. If by attending this ceremony, your child or anyone else in attendance will believe you have somehow come to the conclusion that her sin is no longer an issue, then one of two things needs to happen. Either you have a kind, loving, and compassionate conversation wherein you let your child know your perspective has not changed, but you are willing to be there for her because you love her—not because you support her decision. Alternatively, you may respectfully decline the invitation and let her know you simply cannot attend. For you, maybe you can't attend because the emotional pain of it would be too great. Or maybe it would be an outright violation of your faith and conscience. Let her know that you love her and desire the best for her no matter what! Let her know you respect her right to make this decision, even if you cannot support the decision itself.

Some other things to consider in attending the ceremony:

- Will a Christian minister/pastor be officiating?
- Will the ceremony be held in a church?
- Are your child and his/her partner Christians? (Those who are not yet Christians are not held to the same expectation where sin is concerned.)
- Do any of the elements of the ceremony mention God's blessing over this couple?
- Will you be expected to participate in the ceremony (e.g. giving the bride away)?

Another option is to forgo the ceremony but attend the reception.

Again, it is important to think through the implications of such a decision. Will you be willing to be in the photographs with him and his partner? Will you be willing to take part in the traditional roles of the parents at wedding receptions (e.g. father/daughter dance)? Will it be a traditional reception?

Before making any decision, pray and ask God to direct your thoughts and your decision, to give you wisdom and discernment, and to give you the right words to communicate your heart to your child, regardless of what you decide. The conversation may come down to a discussion about identity. Presumably, your child identifies as a homosexual and you identify as a Christian. Ask your child, *"Knowing how important your identity is to you, would you then have me violate my own identity?"* At the very least, perhaps there can be mutual respect for one another's designated identity. Another way to ask the question might be to say, *"Would you have me violate my faith by celebrating something that is so contrary to who I am?"*

You may ask, *"What if they say, "If you love me, you will attend my wedding.""* You might answer, *"If you love me, you will not ask me to violate my conscience or to compromise who and Whose I am."* Asking for mutual respect of identity and personhood is reasonable and it is a boundary. Remember, boundaries are about helping us to operate in true and real freedom and in our authentic nature as new creations in Christ.

Another consideration is the possibility that refusing to attend the ceremony might damage your relationship beyond repair. Doing so may be more than your child can forgive, and it may cost you any future relationship with her. As with all aspects of your relationship, prayerfully seek God's guidance, pursue wise counsel from a godly friend or professional who is familiar with these issues, and trust God to lead you in your decisions. Do your part, in dependence upon Him. Surrender your will to Him, count the cost, and then do what you believe He is leading you to do. Finally, trust Him with the outcomes. He is trustworthy.

Truthfully, no matter how well you couch this conversation, the likelihood is that your child will be very hurt, which may damage your relationship. At that point, the question for you to answer comes down to: Will you err on the side of compassion, thereby compromising your faith, or will you stand firm in your faith and risk alienating your child? As harsh as it may sound, we are called to please God, not man (I Thessalonians 2:4). If you trust God enough to stand firm in your faith, He will honor that. How? I don't know. However, it may be that God can use the pain produced by this experience to create a godly sorrow in your child that leads to repentance. As Proverbs 27:6 states: *"Wounds from a friend can be trusted...."* Do you trust God and love your daughter enough to let her be wounded, in the hopes that someday she will be delivered from homosexuality? This is one of the toughest questions any parent ever has to answer. May God be with you and direct you as you seek His will for your family.

Q. *Should I pay for their same-sex union?*

A. If attending the same-sex civil union would express approval, paying for the wedding would communicate that to an even higher degree—even if you deny it verbally to her. I don't know if it is even possible to separate support of your relationship with your daughter from a show of approval in this situation. Again, however, only you can make this decision. Seek to please God and to obey Him first—above pleasing your child—and trust Him with the outcomes.

Q. *How does God view divorce between same-sex couples?*

A. As previously discussed, Biblical marriage is between one man and one woman. God stated that those who are married (in the biblical sense) become "one flesh," meaning they are bound together as one unit made up of two individuals, and this union is intended to be lifelong. Because same-sex unions are not sanctioned in Scripture, there are no specific Scriptures speaking to divorce of same-sex couples. Further, because those unions are based upon sexual behavior that is repeatedly condemned in Scripture, we can deduce that divorce does not have the same implications for same-sex couples as it does for heterosexual couples. Divorce, then, becomes a civil proclamation rather than a spiritual one.

It is important to note, however, that because a civil divorce between same-sex couples can be extremely painful for all parties concerned, we recommend approaching these difficult situations with Christ-like love, compassion, empathy, and support, the same as you would a heterosexual child going through a divorce. This is a vital opportunity to show your unconditional love and support to him. He is most likely hurting deeply. Be Jesus to him. Never say, "I told you so." The mandate here is to "...mourn with those who mourn" (Romans 12:15).

However, the spiritual implications are different in these situations. Because these unions are based upon same-sex desire/behavior, which is a distortion of God's intention for sex and marriage, they cannot bless the heart of God. As parents of same-sex attracted children, our goals should be to love our children where they are, yet to pray for them to be set free from Same-Sex Attraction and sexual sin, regardless of our civil laws. *God loves us as we are, but He loves us too much to leave us that way.* He desires so much better for us. His best is *the* best for our children. Remember He is able to redeem any situation for His purposes when we love Him and surrender our wants, desires, and perceived rights to Him. (Romans 8:28). No human condition is beyond God's ability to redeem, for His glory and for our good.

Q. Can those with SSA be healed?

A. Yes! According to God's Word, He is our Creator, He is All-Knowing, Ever Present, and All-Powerful, and because His Word is full of examples of lives that have been set free from sin and thus transformed, we know that no human condition is beyond His ability to redeem it. There is no wound He cannot heal, no heart He cannot change, and no life He cannot restore or reclaim.

We also recognize that <u>we</u> are equally *in*capable of changing anyone. Therefore, as parents, we must surrender our children to the trustworthy hands of God, never ceasing to ask Him to heal our children's wounds, to set them free from this bondage to sin and the deceptions of the enemy, and to transform their lives. Because SSA behavior *is* a sin, we know it is not His will. Thus, we can pray with confidence in His ability to heal and set our children free, while also honoring His timing with patient endurance (Isaiah 49:8; 2 Peter 3:8-9).

Does this mean God will deliver our children from the bondage of homosexuality? Sadly, no. Entrusting our children to Him means we have to submit to His plans and purposes, His timetable, and His perfect will. Not all of our children will be rescued from the homosexual lifestyle, but ultimately our hope must rest in God, not in our children. We hold onto the hope that He will deliver them, even when everything and everyone around us speaks to the contrary.

Finally, we must also recognize that only those who want to be set free will be set free, one way or another. Either God will remove their SSA completely and restore heterosexual desire to them, or He will provide a way for them to experience fulfillment and joy within a heterosexual relationship without removing SSA. Remember, nothing is impossible when we surrender all to Christ. This awareness provides instruction for how we are to pray for our children as follows below. Specifically, we should pray that He will soften their hearts and restore to them a desire to please and honor Him in everything, and as a result, that they will surrender their sexuality completely to Him. As we pray for our children, we must also submit to God's timing as mentioned above.

Our Great and Mighty God knows their wounds. He knows what they need. And He knows what things need to happen in their lives to bring about the transformation of their hearts and minds. As we submit to His will and authority over our children, we are able to move out of His way and come alongside Him as He works in their lives. Our part is to obey Him, trust Him, stand in the gap for our children, and seek to please and honor Him above all else, knowing that His way is best. He will see us through.

Q. *How do I pray for my child with SSA?*

A. First and foremost, pray God would teach you what to pray, by His Holy Spirit within you. Each situation and set of circumstances is different; therefore, we need to ask Him how to pray each time we go before His throne of grace (Hebrews 4:15-16). However, below are some general guidelines to follow when praying for your SSA child.

- Ask God to bring your daughter back to Him—in Spirit and in truth! Whether He restores natural sexuality to her or not, *the* most important thing is that her heart becomes His once again (or for the first time). Once she surrenders her heart (and her sexuality) to Him, the rest of these things will more readily fall into place. Of utmost importance is her relationship with God.

- Ask God to heal your son's wounds.

- Ask Him to give him a desire, first and foremost, for righteousness (right living before God) and second, for a desire for heterosexual attraction to replace Same-Sex Attraction. God is able to transform hearts and lives for His glory. Ask Him to give your son a desire for God-honoring sexuality.

- Ask God to give your daughter sensitivity to her sin (a sensitive conscience) and a desire for a heterosexual relationship.

- Ask God to forgive your son's sins.

- Ask God to silence the deceptive voices of the enemy (Satan), of her own fleshly desire, and of the world and all its influences, and to replace his lies with God's truth.

- Ask Him to guard your son's heart and mind in Christ Jesus and to give him the mind of Christ.

- Ask God to attune your daughter's heart, mind, body, and hearing to His voice by virtue of His Spirit.

- Ask God to be relentless in His pursuit of your son's heart, and to orchestrate the circumstances in his life to turn him away from SSA/SSA behavior and toward Jesus and the life He desires for him.

- Ask God to strengthen the bond with your daughter according to His design, and to continually protect and improve your relationship with her.

- Pray for your child's partner in all these same ways.

- Pray for the relationship with her partner to move toward either a platonic friendship or for their affections for each other to dissolve away completely—according to His will for both their lives.

- Ask God to set your son free from the bondage of Same-Sex Attraction and sexual sin, to have a godly sorrow over his sin that leads him to repentance and to right relationship with Him.

- Trust God to work in her life, knowing that He has her best interests at heart.

- Pray diligently. Pray daily. Pray believing God can and will do what is best according to His plans and purposes.

Q. *How do I pray for my child's other parent and myself?*

A. Ask God to give you His wisdom, insight, heart, and mind for every detail and circumstance regarding your child's sexuality. Ask Him to change your heart and mind in any way He sees fit. Ask Him what He wants to do in your heart and life through this circumstance. Ask God to show you where you have sinned or are sinning in your thoughts, perceptions, or dealings with your child in any way, and especially in regard to sins that are currently hurting your relationship with her. Ask Him to give you the words to speak to your daughter in every encounter you have with her and to put a guard over your mouth when you would say anything that is not in line with His heart (Psalm 141:3). Ask Him to give you a willingness to surrender your hopes, dreams, desires, and wishes for your son to Him, and to make that surrender complete.

Whether you are still married to your child's father/mother or not, pray for him or her, as well as for any step-parents involved, in accordance with the things you are praying for yourself.

Q. *My child and his partner want to adopt/have a child! What should I do?*

A. There are three primary things you must remember in this situation. First, you have no control over what decisions your child and his partner make. You must relinquish whatever perceived or desired control you would like to have in the situation, and entrust every aspect of it to God. The only person you can change is you. Ask God how He would have you respond to this situation. If your child and his partner do indeed adopt a child, that child will be an innocent life, one of the least of these.... (Matthew 24:31-46). If you have the opportunity to love that child, do so with all the love you have to offer. Ask God to show you how He cherishes that child and to pour His love for that child into your heart. If that child comes into your life, God has a purpose in it. Just as you choose to love your child's partner, love the child they adopt. It may not be the way you envisioned or hoped to have a grandchild, but children are a gift from the Lord (Psalm 127:3 NLT). Treat this child in that manner.

Second, pray and ask God to intervene in the situation according to His sovereign will. Then trust Him to do so. If He prevents the adoption (or pregnancy), comfort your son and his partner with sincere love and compassion. If God allows it, trust that He has a purpose in doing so, and endeavor to cooperate with Him in it, according to His will.

Third, remember that God often allows difficult situations to come into our lives because He has a purpose for them. Oftentimes He has *many* purposes in them! Ask Him what His purposes are in bringing this child into your life. Is there something in your heart He wants to change? Is this child a blessing from Him that you would not have otherwise experienced? Does this child need someone like you in his or her life? God has the ability to bring good from even the worst circumstances when we entrust those circumstances to Him (Romans 8:28). Whatever happens has been allowed by God to occur. Trust His wisdom and His plan. Press into Him with your disappointments and your hurts. Lean into Him for strength, wisdom, discernment, and hope. Let Him have His way, especially when you don't understand.

Q. My child is having suicidal thoughts (or thoughts of self-harm). What should I do?

A. First and foremost, whenever your son or daughter (or anyone, for the matter) shares with you that they are having these types of thoughts, *thank them* for trusting you with that information. *Recognize* how difficult it was for them to do so; it took a lot of courage on their part. *Tell them* you know that it did. Then, if they shared that they are suicidal, <u>ask them if they have a plan</u>. **This is critical**. Those who are truly serious about committing suicide will most often have a plan in place by the time they tell someone else.

Second, <u>seek professional help</u>. I cannot stress this enough! The suicide rate for these kids is about six times higher than it is for others in their age brackets. **Suicide is a very real threat** to kids and young adults who are struggling with Same-Sex Attraction and/or are living a homosexual lifestyle. Seek counsel from a qualified mental health professional on your own, first. *(See the Suicide Assessment and guide in the Resources section in the Appendix regarding how to choose a qualified mental health professional.)* That person can help you determine what next steps need to be taken. At the very least your child needs to be in therapy with a qualified mental health professional. If the child is a minor, you have the influence and capacity to place her in counseling. If your son or daughter is an adult with a plan, you should contact the authorities. If he or she has no plan, look for opportunities to encourage him/her to pursue counseling—and pray! Pray for those opportunities to arise. Pray for the right words to communicate your concern and for your child to receive them well. Pray for her to be willing to seek professional help. However, **if the situation meets the criteria laid out in the Suicide Assessment* (in the Appendix), do not hesitate to contact someone locally for immediate intervention.**

Third, after you have become aware of these threats to your child's life, regardless of his age, stay aware of potential signs of self-harm, or the presence of suicidal thoughts or intentions. **Familiarize yourself with the common signs that someone is planning to commit suicide.** Look for evidence of self-harm. Let your son know how very much you love him, and how much his life means to you. Do not be afraid to talk with him, but do so in a way that is compassionate, loving, tender, and is about him—not you. Let him know you are always available to talk with him, anytime, night or day, and then be available! Don't say it if you don't mean it, but if you say it you had better mean it! If you fail to be there after promising you will, that kind of disappointment or let down, for someone who is fragile—and especially this cross-section of people who is so intensely sensitive—could be the final straw for her.

I cannot stress enough the need to **take every mention of suicidal thoughts or intentions seriously**, no matter who they come from. Believe them. Intervene for them (in the ways outlined above), and intercede for them in prayer. They told you for a reason, and often that reason is a cry for help. Be the help or the bridge to help they need.

Q. *My child is misusing drugs/alcohol; what should I do?*

A. Just as with suicidal thoughts or intentions, the threats created by drugs and alcohol use, misuse, or abuse are serious and should be taken seriously. Do not wait for your daughter to have an accident while driving under the influence to voice your concern. If she is a minor, she is your responsibility and should be monitored closely for drugs and alcohol. If you discover she is using, communicate your concern, but also implement checks and balances to ensure her safety. Put strict boundaries in place, and seek professional help in knowing how to safeguard her. Also, get her into therapy with a qualified mental health professional. Our culture is leaning more and more toward the notion that parents of minors have little or no parental authority over their minor children. Do not allow this mindset to intimidate you or to make you feel like you are being overprotective, intrusive, etc., into your daughter's life. God Himself has given you authority over her. Seek Him for wisdom and discernment in how to do that appropriately and for the best interests of your child.

Convincing a minor child to go to counseling is one thing. Getting him to open up to a counselor may be something entirely different! As with other similar scenarios, you only have control over whether or not he goes to counseling. However, you cannot force him to engage in the counseling session.

One of the best things to do when your minor child is resistant to the idea of counseling is to inform any potential mental health professionals that you are interviewing that this is the case. Ask potential counselors about how they deal with minors who are resistant to counseling. How do they draw them out? What has their success rate been? Are they willing to take such a client? Knowing that their sessions with your child are confidential, how will the therapist keep you informed about how the sessions are going without breaking confidentiality? At what point will the counselors concede they are unable to break through to her? These are important questions to ask *before* you hire a therapist. Make sure you and the therapist are on the same page where your daughter's welfare is concerned, and do not hire a therapist whose answers to these questions do not satisfy you. Trust your instincts and the Holy Spirit within you to choose the right mental health professional for her. And trust God with your daughter's heart and with the therapeutic process. The "right" therapist will have experience and a positive track record with resistant children dealing with these issues. What is impossible with man is possible with God (Luke 18:27)! *(See the guide for choosing a qualified mental health professional in the Appendix.)*

If your son is an adult, as with the suicide and self-harm issues, come alongside him, and show him the care and concern you have for him. Offer to be there for him anytime he needs to talk. Let him know how much he means to you, but remember that as an adult his choices are his own. Prayer is the most powerful and effective tool we have in every situation, but most importantly, when we have no control over the other person (James 5:16). Seek God's wisdom and discernment for your son, and intervene in committed, regular prayer on his behalf.

Q. My minor child has been going to counseling because we are making him, but he refuses to participate. The therapist believes it is time to discontinue this therapy relationship. What should I do?

A. Having a mental health professional tell you he has been unable to break through to your daughter is a hard thing to hear, but it is better for the therapist to be honest with you, rather than to continue seeing her. Besides the financial burden this can create, it can also damage her perspective of therapy and may hinder her from seeking this type of help as she grows older.

When this situation arises, you have a couple of options. You can either seek out a different therapist for your daughter, or you can enlist the help of an adult mentor or friend that she trusts and respects. Of course, this person must be someone you also trust and respect. Sometimes such a friend or mentor can make tremendous strides with your daughter when no one else has been able to. Seek God's guidance when this is the case, and trust Him to bring the right person into her life. It may be someone she already knows, or it may be someone new, but at the very least this person must be on the same page with you regarding a Biblical perspective of homosexuality. As with a therapist, maintain close communication with the mentor about your daughter's progress, but respect her privacy. Do not press the mentor for details that would potentially damage her trust of this mentor.

Sometimes, the mentor will be sufficient to support and encourage your son toward growth and stability in facing his SSA challenges. Other times the mentor can be a stepping-stone to a therapeutic relationship down the road. Again, trust God to lead you through this process.

This list of questions is in no way exhaustive. You may, and probably will have more questions at some point down the line. When that happens, please feel free to email us at uncommonloveonline@gmail. com. You and your struggles with the issues surrounding SSA and homosexuality are important to us. We are here for you.

COUNSELING VERSUS COACHING
WHAT YOU NEED TO KNOW

What's the Difference?

Coaching is somewhat of a new profession and many people are uncertain what professional coaching entails and how it differs from counseling/therapy. In the simplest terms, *counseling deals with healing the past*, whereas *coaching helps you move forward from where you are*.

Licensed Professional Counselors

Psychoanalysis (or therapy) is a highly regulated profession with strict educational and licensing requirements and APA guidelines. It can be executed by way of a variety of models. Some of those models include psychoanalysis and psychodynamic therapies, cognitive therapy, humanistic therapy, and integrative or holistic therapies.

An important aspect to note regarding counseling or therapy is that the current APA guidelines require licensed therapists to treat Same-Sex Attraction, homosexuality, and transgender issues as normal. They are required to validate those feelings, emotions, and tendencies in individuals experiencing them. Because of these requirements, some licensed professional counselors are giving up their licenses and opting to transition into life coaching instead. Another alternative to counseling with a licensed professional counselor might be to locate a seasoned Biblical or Christ-centered Christian counselor.

Certified Professional Life Coaches

Because life coaching is a relatively new profession, there are currently no regulatory standards or requirements regarding any aspect of coaching. For that reason, you should be careful who you hire to coach you. (Literally anyone can call themselves a coach!) However, the International Coaching Federation (ICF) has created professional standards for those wishing to obtain Certified Professional Life Coach

(CPLC) credentials. Those pursuing their CPLC must meet a standard of professional training which includes: completing a certain number of instructional hours of training with an approved ICF school, passing an exam, and completing a practicum. For this reason, it would be wise to only hire a coach with a CPLC or higher certification, and one approved by the ICF.

To recap:

- Counseling is about healing the past, while coaching is about moving forward from where you are today.

- Licensed professional counselors are now required by the APA to affirm SSA, homosexuality, and transgender thoughts, feelings, and identifications.

- Coaches who have obtained their CPLC by an approved ICF school are professionally trained to help you with your coaching needs.

*Contact us at Uncommon Love Ministries (*uncommonloveonline@ gmail.com*) for more information.*

How to Choose a Qualified Mental Health Professional

1. Ask friends and family for referrals. This can be the quickest way to find a counselor who is a good fit for you. However, if you don't feel this person is right for you, don't feel obligated to choose this person. Everyone has different things they look for in a therapist. Your friends or family may have had different criteria than you, and that's okay. Do what is best for you.

2. Shop online for prospects in your area. You can find out a lot about therapists in your area by looking on the Internet. Check for their areas of specialty, education and training, certification, and anything that may tell you about their ideology or faith. Look for professionalism in both their biography and their photo.

3. Choose the appropriate gender according to what you perceive is best *for the client*. If your child or you are more comfortable talking with a male, look for a male therapist. If the preference is for a female, look for a woman.

4. Call them or set up a time to meet them. Following are some good questions to ask:

   - Where did he go to school? The thing to look for is that the therapist graduated from an accredited school and not an online certification program.

   - Is he licensed? Look up the license to make sure. There are people who don't have a license and are practicing. Once you verify he actually has a license, look on the state licensing boards to see if there are any infractions against the license.

- Is she a Christian therapist? What does that mean to her? Where does she stand on the issue of homosexuality? Does she have training in biblical counseling? If so, from where?

- Has he worked with people with the issues in question? On the phone, share a little about your presenting issue and see how the therapist responds. Make sure the therapist you choose holds to beliefs that are in line with yours (and God's Word) about whatever issues you want to address.

- What is her training? If she says she is trained, find out if it was a one-day seminar in EMDR, and/or, whether she took a three-hour online course in psychoanalysis. If she calls herself an expert in a modality after such a short training, move on to someone with a little more experience.

5. Ask about the fee and discuss the potential for a sliding scale or insurance. If you like everything about the person, but the rate is more than you can manage, tell him so. If he can slide no lower, ask for referrals. He might know someone who works like he does for a lower fee. That said, you often get what you pay for, so if at all possible, don't allow finances alone to determine whom you hire.

6. Notice how you feel during your discussion with the therapist. If you're nervous or anxious, does she help to alleviate those feelings, make them worse, or have no impact on them? Is she dynamic and energetic or calm and perceptive? Does she listen and hear you well? Was she defensive about any of the questions you asked? Is she trying too hard to 'sell' her services to you, or does she seem to be more concerned that you have a counselor who is a good fit for you? Assess these same things after your first session with her. If you decide that she isn't a good match, then you don't need

to go back. Let her know that and why, if you feel comfortable doing so.

7. Look for any red flags such as ethical issues, boundary issues, faith issues, etc. If you see any red flags, keep searching.

BE AWARE: Licensed professional counselors are now required by the APA to affirm and validate SSA, homosexuality, and transgender thoughts, feelings, and identifications.

Suicide Assessment and Response

Assess suicide risk by asking the following questions in a calm manner.

1. Have you had thoughts of harming yourself? Can you tell me something about that? *(Thought)*

2. Are you still thinking about harming yourself? *(Persistent or repeated thought)*

3. Have you thought about how you plan to do this? *(Plan)*

4. When do you plan on doing this? *(Imminence)*

5. Do you have or can you get access to the items you need to carry out your plan? *(Ability)*

If his/her answers are affirmative, the potential of suicide is real and the need for professional assessment is **immediate**. You **must respond** to the suicidal person by attempting to get him/her help – whether voluntary or involuntary on his/her part.

1. If you're talking to the person on the phone, try your best to get his/her present location.

2. Make a plan with the person about taking him/her to a hospital or a professional for suicide assessment immediately.

3. Take every threat or discussion of self-harm or suicide seriously. When in doubt about whether or not to report, err on the side of intervening in the person's life.

Emergency Contact Information:

- Police/Sheriff: 9-1-1

- Suicide Prevention Hotline: 1-800-273-TALK (8255) or 1-800-SUICIDE (784-2433)

  - TTY: 799-4TTY (4889)

  - Ayuda En Español Prevencion de Suicidio - 888-628-9454

  - Website: https://suicidepreventionlifeline.org/

For Assistance in Your Area, Google the Following:

- Police non-emergency
- Police crime prevention
- County Health Dept.
- Crisis Assessment Center
- Local Hospital ER

ABOUT THE AUTHOR

Mary Comm has been in Christian ministry for almost 20 years. She is an experienced Christian Ministry Director, Author, Speaker, and Certified Professional Life Coach. Mary is a gifted and caring leader whose passion is to help Christians navigate the painful circumstances of life in the healthiest and best ways possible, honoring God and restoring joy even in the midst of unspeakable hurt and brokenness. She is the author of <u>Secret Sin: When God's People Choose Abortion</u> (Morgan James Publishing, 2006) and <u>Building Bridges: Paving the Way for Partnering with the Churches in Your Area</u> (Morgan James Publishing 2008). She has also published an e-book titled, <u>Why Do Bad Things Happen? (And Where is God When They Do?)</u> (Amazon Publishing 2015). Mary is a seasoned and compassionate small group leader and professionally trained and certified Life Coach.

Mary became involved in abortion recovery and awareness after having been an accomplice to an abortion. In 1996, she founded *SafeHaven Ministries, Inc.,* an online peer-support site for the abortion-minded and those traumatized by abortion, and in 2003 she established *In Our Midst Ministries,* another 501(c)-3 ministry focused on raising awareness in the Church regarding the prevalence of abortion trauma among Christian families. Mary has been featured on various radio programs including *Focus on the Family's* <u>Family News in Focus</u> and Moody Radio's <u>Midday Connection,</u> as well as *Gospel of Life* and *Facing Life Head On* television programs. Mary holds a Bachelor of Science in Psychology and a Biblical Studies Certificate, both from Colorado Christian University, as well as a CPLC, obtained through Christian Coach Institute, an approved International Coach Federation (ICF) institution. She resides in Thornton, Colorado.

Other Books by Mary Comm

Secret Sin: When God's People Choose Abortion
ISBN: 978-1600371486 Morgan James Publishing, LLC (2006)

Building Bridges, Paving the Way for Partnering with the Churches in Your Area

**A Guide for Pregnancy Resource Centers, Abortion Recovery Ministries,
& Others Involved in the LIFE Issue**
ISBN: 978-60037-410-4 Morgan James Publishing, LLC (2008)

Why Do Bad Things Happen? (And Where is God When They Do?)

Exploring Two of Life's Hardest Questions
ASIN: B00ZZ2D6EU Kindle Edition (2015)

~ BONUS OFFERS ~

1. **Free One-Hour Introductory Coaching Session to the first 50 people to submit a request at uncommonloveonline@gmail.com.**

    This one-hour coaching session includes a free discovery session and assessments. This free coaching session is for new clients only and must be scheduled and completed prior to December 31, 2019. Potential topics for coaching include:

    *   Setting and enforcing healthy boundaries
    *   Restoring your relationship
    *   Marital issues, step-parenting, etc.
    *   Overcoming fear; finding hope
    *   Overcoming guilt and shame
    *   Pinpointing and engaging in healthy self-care
    *   General help with current issues with your son or daughter
    *   When you simply need someone safe to talk to….

2. **Free Uncommon Love Facilitator's Guide to the first 50 people who attend facilitator training.**

    Our Facilitator's Guide is due to be completed by fall of 2018. We plan to begin scheduling facilitator trainings in August of 2018. These trainings are for anyone who wishes to lead an Uncommon Love Bible Study Support group, either through their local church or small group.

3. **Free one-year membership to the Uncommon Love Private Facebook group for the first 50 people to submit their request via email at uncommonloveonline@gmail.com.**

    LIMIT: One Bonus offer per person.

Contact Information

Uncommon Love Ministries
PO Box 33794
Northglenn, CO 80233

URL: http://uncommonlove.online
Email: uncommonloveonline@gmail.com
Facebook: https://www.facebook.com/uncommonloveonline

End Notes

1 http://www.apa.org/advocacy/civil-rights/sexual-diversity/index.aspx

2 https://www.goodreads.com/quotes/60503-he-saw-you-cast-into-a-river-of-life-you

3 https://www.goodreads.com/quotes/60503-he-saw-you-cast-into-a-river-of-life-you

4 Cohen, Richard, Gay Children, Straight Parents; A Plan for Family Healing: A Plan for Family Healing (CreateSpace Independent Publishing Platform, 2016) 72-75

5 Cohen, Richard, Gay Children, Straight Parents; A Plan for Family Healing: A Plan for Family Healing (CreateSpace Independent Publishing Platform, 2016) 72-75

6 Johnson, Barbara; Where Does A Mother Go To Resign? (Bethany House Publishers; Reissue edition, 1979)

7 Worthen, Anita & Davies, Bob Someone I Love is Gay; How Family & Friends Can Respond (IVP Books, 1996)

8 Johnson, Barbara; Where Does A Mother Go To Resign? (Bethany House Publishers; Reissue edition, 1979)

9 http://www.suicidology.org/Portals/14/docs/Resources/LGBT%20Resources/LGBTresource-sheet.pdf

10 Warren, Rick, Daily Hope with Rick Warren https://www.facebook.com/permalink.php?story_fbid=742945089094933&id=488407254548719 July 5, 2014

11 Eldredge, John, Waking the Dead: The Glory of a Heart Fully Alive (Thomas Nelson Inc, 2006)

12 Eldredge, John, Waking the Dead: The Glory of a Heart Fully Alive (Thomas Nelson Inc, 2006)

13 Cohen, Richard, Gay Children, Straight Parents: A Plan for Family Healing (CreateSpace Independent Publishing Platform, 2016)

14 Cohen, Richard, Gay Children, Straight Parents: A Plan for Family

Healing (CreateSpace Independent Publishing Platform, 2016)

15 https://www.goodreads.com/work/quotes/513960-the-language-of-letting-go-hazelden-meditation-series

16 https://www.ncbi.nlm.nih.gov/pubmed/22048730

17 Cloud, Henry and Townsend, John, Boundaries Updated and Expanded Edition: When to Say Yes, How to Say No To Take Control of Your Life (Zondervan, 2017)

18 https://www.goodreads.com/work/quotes/513960-the-language-of-letting-go-hazelden-meditation-series

19 http://www.suicidology.org/Portals/14/docs/Resources/LGBT%20Resources/LGBTresource-sheet.pdf

20 Jernigan, Dennis, Renewing Your Mind: Identity and the Matter of Choice (Innovo Publishing, 2017)

21 Jernigan, Dennis, Renewing Your Mind: Identity and the Matter of Choice (Innovo Publishing, 2017)

Morgan James
Speakers Group

www.TheMorganJamesSpeakersGroup.com

We connect Morgan James published authors with live and online events and audiences who will benefit from their expertise.

Printed in the USA
CPSIA information can be obtained
at www.ICGtesting.com
JSHW022324140824
68134JS00019B/1276